Killing the Sky

ORAL HISTORIES
FROM HORIZON ACADEMY,
RIKERS ISLAND
NUMBER 2

Killing the Sky: Oral Histories from Horizon Academy, Rikers Island

Number 2

ISBN: 1-932948-19-8

Classroom Teachers: Freebbie Rivera Jr., Josh Gray, John Parada

SPI Curriculum Consultant: Erick Gordon

Teaching Artists/Oral Historians: Kerry McKibbin, Vickie Ndibo, Lalitha Vasuvdevan

Guest Teachers: Katherine Cincotta, Jim Fenner

Book Design: Paul Wein

Photographs: Katherine Cincotta, Jim Fenner, Erick Gordon

For more information about SPI, please contact:

Student Press InitiativeTeachers College, Columbia University

Box 182

525 West 120th Street

New York, NY 10027

ergordon@tc.edu

www.publishspi.org

ACKNOWLEDGEMENTS

This project would not have been possible without the support and guidance of Horizon Academy's Principal, Ms. Gloria Ortiz and the G.R.V.C Department of Correction.

Additionally, we would like to offer our gratitude to Warden Larry Davis, Deputy Warden of Programs Hakim S. El-Quhir, Senior Superintendent Tim Lisante, D.O.C. Director of Education, Ms. Francis Torres and G.R.V.C. Site Coordinator, Leila Riley.

A special acknowledgment goes out to Officer Climent, Officer Robeson, Officer Martin, Site Coordinator Juan Frias, Supervisor of Instruction Sandy Roter, Social Worker Cesar Vera, Ronnye Hightower, Stacey Oliger and Mary Runyan.
Lastly, many thanks are owed to the officers, G.R.V.C teachers and hard-working students at Horizon Academy.

CONTENTS

FOREWORD

Jim Fenner, Erick Gordon, Kerry McKibbin, Vickie Ndibo, Lalitha Vasudevan

Storytelling is a powerful act. Stories are how we come to understand each other, share differences and find common ground. Stories are the keepers of our histories and the foundation for our futures. So what are the stories we hear from or about young men who are incarcerated? How do we form understandings of their lives? And in what ways might we include their voices, experiences, and insights into our interpretations and understandings of the world?

The voices, memories, and imagined futures reproduced in this volume are the result of eight young men's decision to share their stories with an unknown audience. They represent eight lives that began across the world and converged at Rikers Island, New York, which is where we (the collaborators/writing mentors/editors of this collection) met and worked together with them to bring their spoken words onto the printed page.

We developed a method of working intended to enfranchise those students for whom traditional definitions of teaching and learning have failed. The young men's stories began as spoken conversations and evolved through further dialogue within themselves, with each other and with us. Over the course of three months of writing, editing, and recollecting, we worked to bring this collection of stories to fruition. This was a process of working that challenged their commonly held assumptions about where education exists and how learning happens.

Their words paint images of familial love, disappointment, support; friendships and relationships; mentorship and role-models. Theirs are lives and experiences inflected by hard-won lessons from unexpected places. Through their narratives, these authors can regain mobility in meaning, giving foot to stories that are otherwise relegated to audiences of cement walls and corrugated bars. Throughout the process of creating this book, several of the participants expressed a desire for their stories to reach a vast audience that included current elementary, middle and high school students. Imagine the paths these stories might travel—touching lives and reaching further than their teller will ever know.

That's All I'll Tell Him

Phat Boi

My name is Phat Boi. I was born on October 4th, 1984 in a hospital in Flushing, Queens. New York Hospital, that's what it was called. All my life I lived in Queens. I grew up in Corona, Queens. When I was young I really didn't go out much. When I moved to another place in Corona, when I was like maybe in fourth or fifth grade, that's when I started hanging out with bigger crowds. Every corner there were a lot of people hanging out.

TO HAVE EVERYTHING

I have a sister and there are two other boys—one older brother and another younger one. I'm the middle. And I have a small little sister. Right now she's thirteen. My younger brother is seventeen, and my older brother's 23.

I grew up with both my mom and dad. My dad, he's just a workingman. I wake up, he's not there. I go to sleep, he's not there. He wakes up in the morning and comes home after I sleep, and he tries not to wake me up. He's

been working for UPS for ten years now. My mother used to work in Manhattan making jewelry. She used to make earrings, necklaces, chokers, stuff like that. She made stuff that the stores would buy from the factory. My mom was always home. She used to bring the stuff home to make it in the house, and then she'd bring it to the factory and pick up more. So basically she used to make the earrings and all the necklaces and things in the house. Both of them worked a lot to pay the bills and keep us in good shape.

When I was a kid, I always wanted the new sneakers. I was in love with sneakers since I was a kid. Every sneaker that came out–from Jordans, to Up-Towns, to Nikes. I couldn't have the sneakers when I wanted them when I was younger because it was four of us. So my mom would just take turns buying us stuff. It was type-rough when I was young. Basically I was living good. I always had food, clothes. But I always wanted to be the person to have everything. I would go to stores and see the clothes I always wanted, but I couldn't have. That's when I started. I got a little older and I was cutting, trying to make money. I started selling street products at a young age.

INTO THAT TRAP

I was, like, maybe thirteen when I started selling. Everybody where I lived was older. I had an older cousin on the block, so he introduced me to everybody. I was selling drugs at a young age but I didn't start partying and smoking at a young age. One day I was cutting school at my friend's house and everybody there was smoking. And they were like, "Yo, come on. Let's go smoke," and I was like, "Nah." I always kept away from it. And one day there was this girl. I was mad for some reason, she was with her friends and they were smoking and she was like, "Come on." And so it was my first shot and I didn't say no. She was my girlfriend at the time. And from that day I just started smoking like, basically, at fifteen years old. I would take my girl out and I'd always waste money on her. My mother used to ask me, "Ooh, how are you getting all this?" I told her it was my friend's, or I told her my girl bought me things.

My parents were mad at me but basically they got fed up with it, they just left it alone. "Alright, this is your life, you do what you want to do. Just remember that you gonna regret it." My mother was always there for me. She did everything. She gave me so much grace, I can't count it no more. When I stopped going to school, she never told my father. When I got suspended from school, she never told my father. She caught me smoking cigarettes, and she never told my father. If he would've known, he would have been mad at me. He would have started screaming at me. Not hit me, because I never got hit by my parents. But they'd scream at me and they'd punish me. Or they wouldn't give me no money. They wouldn't buy me what I need.

My mother knew what it was but she never threw it in my face. I don't know why she never threw it in my face, but I know she knew. One day she found some weed in my room in a Ziploc bag I had left on top of the radio. And she was like, "What is this?" She was asking, "What is this?" She was like, "I know, I know y'all guys smoking but don't have it in my house. Don't disrespect my house. You're already old enough. I could kick you out of here." I was still livin' at the house. But she said, you know, don't disrespect the house. I respected that, but I told her it wasn't mine. I told her it was my friend's—I was just holding it. I regret all that. Because, basically, I smoked so much that sometimes I forget—like in school? I stopped going to school because I was smoking. And I stopped doing a lot of things because I was smoking and getting high. Sometimes I had to go to an appointment for the school because I was just getting kicked out of school so much. I forgot about school, and I was just partying with all my friends who smoked weed. So I missed a lot of things. My mom is mad about it. She doesn't agree with it at all. She never smoked. I've never seen my father or my mother smoke.

I would change that first time that I started smoking because since I started smoking I stopped going to school. The last grade I attended was tenth. I finished ninth and I was starting tenth. I went to New Town High School in Elmhurst, Queens. I'd wake up early to be there for first period, but I'd just stay outside the whole day making money. I sold drugs outside of my school. And then after that—after I got kicked out of that school—I had a lot of other appointments for LaGuardia, for West Side High School. But I was so into making money, the money was so good, that I just didn't want to go to school. I just didn't go. When I was younger, I tried to get jobs but the money I was making in the job wasn't the same money I was making in the street.

I always regret smoking because when I used to smoke I used to forget a lot of stuff. Like when I'm in school now, I really know how to do it but I need to review it because I forgot the steps. I always used to be quick. If the teacher gave us a worksheet, I would always want to be the first one done with all the right questions. That's the effect marijuana has; it makes you forget. That's what I regret. If I had never smoked, I woulda been better. I still could change my life because I'm only 21. I still could change it. But if I would have kept full-on with school, everything would be good. I wouldn't, who knows, I wouldn't never have been here. Now I'm not smoking, so now I'm good. That's why when I get out I'm just going to do what I have to do. I'm not going to start. I'm not going to fall into that trap again.

COOKIE

I was basically a good student. I was a good student all through elementary school, junior high, and high school. In high school, I started slacking a little. I went to IS145 and then I went to 204 'cause at 145 I got kicked

out of the school. One day I went to class and I was giving the teacher my homework and he, like, shoved me. So then I just turned around and I threw a chair. I missed. I should have never done that, but he should have never put his hands on me. That day I wasn't feeling good. I don't know. I probably woke up on the wrong side of the bed. So, yeah, they kicked me out of the school.

Then I went to IS204. They said I had a short temper and all this other stuff. They thought I had some type of problem so they put me in Special Ed. I had counseling first, and then I had Special Ed but I was too smart for Special Ed so they put me in regular classes. I'd go to counseling and the counselor would ask me all types of questions. He would try to find out, well, why I did what I did. Why did I toss the chair at the teacher? He always asked me about that. He always asked if I had problems at home. "Is your parents right with you? How they treat you?" and I would tell him, "Good, good." It was hard for him to find out the problem, but I told him I have a short temper and I don't like when people touch me, basically. When they touch me or make fun of me, I get mad. I get angered. He'd try to work on anger with me. How to face problems, how to prevent problems.

When I was in junior high school, I walked away from some fights. I wasn't that type that would just fight over nothing. Kids in junior high were jealous because some times I'd just come in with a brand new pair of sneakers and they'd step on me or something. And I'd just leave it alone. I won't do nothing about it. Until one day I just snapped and that's when they thought, "Damn."

There was this one kid, he'd always step on my sneakers. I'm in class and he'd always come, ungh. Where he stepped on my sneakers, they'd get creased and dirty. It was a group of them, and I was by myself, so I left it alone. Until one day we just got into a fight. They tried to jump me but the security guards came along. They waited for me outside of school that day, and the security guards and the principal didn't let me out of the school. And they called my mother. So the next day I came into school, I looked like a wimp because my mother had to come and pick me up. So that next day we fought again. I don't care what people say because they don't know me, but I didn't feel right myself so that's why the next day in the morning we fought across the street in the park before going to school. That was a fair one. It was just me and him—it was one-on-one—and we just fought. He gave me respect. He said, "I respect you 'cause you came up like a man and we fought." The only reason he gave me his respect because I gave him a cookie or black eye, you could say. That's how we call it because it looks like an Oreo cookie. I was like fifteen or sixteen. Fifteen years old.

ALWAYS, EVERY DAY

I dropped out of school when I was seventeen, when I got into high school. That high school was around where I used to live. I knew a lot of people. I knew the whole school, so I just walked in there and I knew everybody.

I had a teacher—Mr. Clifford, I think—in high school. He'd always try to help me. Always. He'd pull me out of class and ask me what's wrong. He'd try and encourage me to pass the class. Always, every day. If I wasn't there, he'd call me at my house. We was very close like that. He was a teacher-slash-dean and sometimes both of the deans and him, they would look out the window and they'd see us smoking or something. And then sometimes I'd go to class smellin' like mad weed. I'd smoke it and just go to class and he'd look at me and I was like... I'd just walk in and do my work. They knew, but they never did anything. I stopped going to counseling because I thought I didn't need no more counseling. When I stopped going to counseling, it was around when I was finishing ninth grade, in the middle of ninth and tenth grade. They never spoke to me about doing drugs. You know how sometimes you've got these classes about "don't do drugs" and this and that? I didn't think of none of that. I was just doing what I had to do.

COPPED OUT

I was like, seventeen when I caught my first case. I copped out to a program, a CASES [Center for Alternative Sentencing and Employment Services] program. I couldn't smoke or nothing because they was taking my urine, and they had to put me in school and I was taking all types of classes. They gave me an internship there. That's when I tried to change my life, the first time I got arrested.

It was a robbery. Me and my friend, we had robbed this guy. When we was walking away, the guy seen a cop on a bike, patrolling, so he stopped him and we got arrested. I spent, maybe, three months fighting the case. They gave me probation and, since I wasn't going to school, they put me in CASES in Manhattan on Canal Street. Once you go there, you've got a case manager who'll take care of you and help you with your problems. That's the first person you see every day. My case manager put me in this internship group and I was in a drug group. I was also in an AIDS group, a sex group. I lived home, but I had to go there every day. I spent four hours a day there. I went every day for maybe six-to-eight months. It was good. I changed my life. They were teaching me how to look for a job, how to approach the manager, how to write a résumé, what are the proper words you speak, stuff like that. And they gave me an internship. I was in this hospital in the central sterile supply. That's like sterilizing the tools before the surgeons use them. I learned a lot from that program but I didn't really change all of my bad ways because I was still selling drugs.

RIP, LOS

When I was eighteen years old, my best friend killed himself 'cause a lot of people envied him. He was like twenty years old. After that happened, I changed my life. I think that if I do what I got to do and keep it on a low key, I could live a better life. RIP, Los.

Before I got locked up, I stopped smoking. I was working. I was going to go to school. But then I got caught up in it again. I just got clean. So I've just got to work and stop hanging out because I hang out a little too much. I knew I should've changed but I was living in the wrong neighborhood. I was in Corona. I had too many friends so everyday I'd come home I'd bump into 'em. When I saw my friends, I just want to be, "Let's go. Whatever you want to do, let's do it. You wanna break night, let's break night. Let's go party. Let's go to a club. Let's go do whatever you want to do. Let's go." That's how it was.

Then I moved from a bad neighborhood to a better one. I'm still in Queens, but I'm in the other side. I'm in Whitestone. But I still go to my old neighborhood 'cause of my girl and I chill with her all the days when I can. But now I live in a quiet neighborhood. There's nobody around. Nobody hangs around the corner. When I go home, I just go straight home, eat something, go to sleep. But before, I was just in the wrong neighborhood. Where I live now, if I was in that neighborhood before, my life would be changed.

AT LEAST TWO OR THREE OF THEM ARE RATS

The reason I dropped out of high school—the main reason—is 'cause I caught this case and I really didn't want to go to school. I was cutting a lot. That's when I got the internship and I stayed working there for a while. And then, after that, I just was hanging out, making money in the street.

I learned a lot on the street 'cause I always hung around with an older group. I never hung around with kids my age that much. That was only when I was in school. They taught me a lot of right from wrong. They told me go to school, but I was never listening. Yeah, they always told me, "Go to school. I don't want to see you on the block during school time." I just cut out somewhere, to somebody's house, and then I'd come back. Basically, they taught me how the street life is. Always give respect. Don't disrespect somebody older

than you. Keep your eye on your own ground. Keep it to yourself. Don't bring a lot of people around because if you bring a lot of people around, at least two or three of them are rats. They might do ya dirty. Like say you're in your house counting money or something. You go use the bathroom, they might take your money. They might do you dirty. They might try to kick it to your girl when you're not around. Might try to rob the crib or something when you not around. That's why they always tell you, keep it to a minimum.

They was telling me how the drug game goes. They told me always have your money straight. Don't waste it. Always re-up before you waste it. When you're out, just cop whatever you need and don't run around just buyin' stuff. There was some moments that I would just throw all the money away, and it was me and my friend goin' half and he would come and say, "Give me some money." I was always like, "I don't know." I got in fights over that. You could say that, to this day, probably the only friend I have now is my girl. I just kick it—it's just me and her. I have a lot of friends I hang out with, but I don't bring them into my personal life.

THAT'S ALL

I've been in too much trouble in my life. I've been in and out of jail like six or seven times so I really don't want to come back here. I'm tired of this. I see people here—50, 60 years old—and I don't want to be them when I get older. I'd rather be somewhere else. I wanna be doin' my own thing when I get older, owning a business, you know. The way I want to go, the way I have to plan, is first I'm gonna call a couple of schools. I could either go back to school or get a G.E.D. if I don't get it here. Or go to a trade school—either a computer school or a cooking school. I could do that for a while, so I'd see what I could achieve from it, and get a job and just keep myself out of trouble. I want to achieve some of my goals and go to school, go to college. Get my degree, somewhere. Just keep myself focused.

See, if I would've listened to my parents in the beginning, everything would have been good. Basically, whatever my parents was telling me when I was growing up, it's true. I always thought it was false, like they was just talking s— and I wasn't believing them or whatever. But if I would've kept on in school, I wouldn't have fallen into the traps I fell in like coming out of jail, getting into fights. The streets, they don't bring nothing but problems. I could've avoided all of that if I had listened to my parents.

I fell in love with this girl. She was the most beautiful girl I ever seen. I knew her for a while but I never said anything to her. But one day, I just asked her if she wanted to go out with me and she said yeah. From there, she changed my whole life around. And 'til this day, I am still in love with her. She's my life. I'm engaged to her. I could live this life with my girl because I've been with her for three and a half years and it's time to move on. I want to build a family with her. When I have a son someday, I'm going to explain my life to him, all the things I've been through. Tell him, "Son, you don't need to go through this. Just do what you've got to do. Go to school and finish. And just think about yourself." I'll always keep reminding him nobody's better than him. He's the best because, if he thinks that somebody's better than him, he's going to want to be like them. He's going to fall into the traps that I fell in. So if he'll grow up saying that he's the best, he'll think he's the best. He won't need nothing in life. That's all I'll tell him.

That's How You Get Around

Jermaine C.

My name is Jermaine C. This is gonna be a first-time experience for me. I never did this before. I'm a guy that loves to write, so by you coming up and giving me the opportunity to write in this book, it really makes me feel good. I love to learn a lot. I feel like I'm very smart. I think learning is very important. It's a good exercise for your brain.

HIDING THE HOMEWORK

When I was young, I didn't like to write at all. I would go to school everyday and the teacher would give me homework that has to do with writing, to do at home. I would come home and hide the homework from my grandmother so I wouldn't have to do it. One day my grandmother was cleaning out my room and she looked under my bed and found all the homeworks I had been hiding from her for the longest. She yelled, "Michael, what is all of this I found under your bed? How come you been hiding your homework from me?"

I answered her, "Grandma, I'm not good at writing." She gave me a beating and told me I was punished for a month.

Learning how to write was, in my eyes, scary, because my grandmother used to beat me a couple of times 'til I got it correct. I had to stay up late at night until I got it, and, in the morning,I had no choice but to go to school tired.

When I used to go to school, the teacher'd be like, "Write a paragraph about this word," or "Write a paragraph about this word," but then you had to… When I started writing paragraphs, I had forgotten how to indent, commas, and how to use a hyphen. I learned that in a paragraph, you have to put them in right order, like the first part is the introduction, last part is conclusion, middle part is like the thing that's like the body, like you tell specifically what the story is really about. Then you come to a conclusion.

A VERY INQUISITIVE PERSON

My grandmother was real strict. She used to teach me how to read, mostly, and she used to sit down and teach me math. She was smart—a very inquisitive person. And she was very suspicious. But she was just like me. She liked to learn, and she thought education was important. She had a good heart. You know, she was a loving and caring person, so I came from a good family. She was very loving and caring, like she was everybody's grandmother. That's how she was.

She was my mama's mom. She lived with me all my life and taught me the rules, like she taught me manners around the table, how to be respectful—a lot of stuff. She taught me to hang out with the right company and not with the wrong company, and don't talk too much. Keep quiet and just listen and don't talk too much, period. It's not good. It's not good to have a lot of company – most of the time you should only have one specific friend, one significant friend. So one friend was good enough. She taught me not to go to people's houses a lot, that that's not good. I'm telling you, you she was a suspicious person.

Where she's from, Jamaica, you know, it's a whole lotta stuff going on out there. People are killed; education is rare. The money rate is low, and it's

hard for people to survive. A lot of people sell drugs out there, and the environment is very poor. She took me there, and I had a good experience with her. She was the first person who put me on a plane. I was nervous 'cause I was young when I went. I was, what, eight? So I would think, "Oh, the plane will probably go upside down." So I was nervous. At the same time, I was happy, like, "Damn, I'm going to the sky, I wanna see how it is!" But at the same time, I thought it might flip upside down like when you watch movies. I thought in my head I might be dying.

I got locked up after she passed, in August 2004. I kinda got a little loose, I felt a little free, but then at the same time, it kinda broke me down to the point where I had to do wrong things. But then as I got locked up, I realized how important education is 'cause it's now cool, know what I'm sayin'? I owe her a lot. She used to stay up every night and worry about me, like, damn, she used to worry sick about me! And I know, you know, I know I killed my grandmother because she wondered where I was at, so I guess she caught a heart attack. Even if I was to get a masters degree, I would still owe my grandmother more than that. My grandmother, you know, she was my best friend. I should have listened to her, so you know. She was really the closest person to me in our family.

BATTLING THEM

The first time I went on a plane, I went to Ohio to see my aunt. She was a good role model – she's Jamaican, and she's a principal at some junior high school. Now, she had these two sons, which is my cousins, smart as hell. I would go over there, and everything had to be strict and everything had to be education-wise and everything was a thinking process, a brain process. She would sit down and teach me how to read – she'd say "Alright, Germaine (my cousin), you read this story and then Jermaine, you read this story, and we'll see who reads quick," and "What does this word mean?" and stuff. Then, you know, they'd get it before me, they'd win the competition. I ran into competition with my cousins and it made my strategies stronger for reading. I used to like battling them. I was eleven.

To be honest, in the beginning it wasn't fun for me because, you know, I knew I wasn't smarter than them. At the same time, alright, now it's a competition going on, so my strategy was getting stronger and I wanted to win, so it became fun. Sometimes they won and sometimes I lost. We'd argue. We'd fight. It'd get, you know, physical, like we'd fight for real, for real. Everything got serious. So, from education to video games – we'd play video games – he'd run a competition with me. His mom would want somebody to go to the store for her, right, and he wanted to go for his mom instead of me. It was a reward to me. I would get a little jealous because I was a visitor there. But, I got smarter in reading.

I WANNA BUST THAT QUESTION OUT

I had a bad experience with math. When I was young, I always been bad with math, I mean, I can't get it, I can't. Every time I would try to, you know, solve a answer, I would fail. That's why I know how to read more better than I know how to, you know, do the math.

I remember one day, I went over to my friend's house and his uncle was there. He retired from being a police officer. So he came over and I sat on the couch in my friend's apartment, and he was asking me and him a question, a math question, and damn! We both tried to figure it out! It was fun, though, because we was running a competition between me and my friend, in me and his eyes – we wanted to see who's smarter. So we try solving the question and whatnot, and then, to be honest, my friend got it right. I don't know.

I like to write. I'm good at writing letters and stuff. I wrote this letter for a friend of mine so he could send it to his girl. He doesn't know how to write a paragraph in the right form, or the way to conversate in a letter – he don't know the right things to say and stuff. So I wrote the letter for him.

Now, I'll sit in my cell all day long and figure out questions that Mr. Gray gave me until what, two o'clock in the morning? He was teaching us how to do fractions and I already knew how to do fractions, but he was teaching me how to reduce fractions. I always had problems with that ever since I was young. We went over the lessons a couple of times and I still couldn't get it. I felt embarrassed because I know I'm smart—I know I'm smart, like, if you give me a question to do but you give me the procedures, the tools, break it down and tell me how to do it, I'll do it. I catch on quick. I went back to my cell at night and went, "Damn!" It gets me mad, but in a way I'm happy I'm getting mad because then I'll wanna bust this question out. It gives me a high, a motive… it gives me a chance to answer the question in the right form. But damn, it just basically broke me down.

So Mr. Gray gave me a couple questions to answer and I worked on it, I just kept working on it. I went over it a couple of times to make sure it's right. I did the whole procedure, I had it packed in my head at first and broke it down, and I came to conclusion, see what I'm sayin'? So I felt good. It made me realize, you know, when I was coming up, I used to cut school a lot. It made me realize how important education is. I love to learn. All you gotta do is keep your ears open, your eyes open, and you'll get through.

My buddy over there helps me in math; he's like my older brother when it comes to math. A very good role model. Ask him anything, he knows it, and he knows how to teach math good, too. Compared to a teacher, he knows how to teach good 'cause he'll break it down to me. We met each other in class. When we first met each other, it was the beginning and math was easy, so I used to get certain questions right. Some of the questions he got wrong, so I used to say, "No, that's not how you do it, you do it like this!" And he'd be like, "Mind your business." We started running a little competition in math and now it gets harder and harder. They're trying to get us stronger in math now, with the G.E.D. book. Some of the questions I can't answer, like the ones I want to know, the hard ones. I like to learn, like I said.

When I was coming up, math was just regular math. Now they got word problems. Say they put a question up on the board that has to do with multiplication. Now, I know how to read it, I get what it's saying, but I don't know that it's multiplication because I don't know what a certain word in the paragraph means to do. Say, John has fifteen candies and he went to the store and bought fifteen more candies, how many candies he have altogether now? You know, that's 30, you add them, but in multiplication, I don't know….

I took the predictor test, and I passed it, so I was going to take the G.E.D. test but I didn't get to it because I was going home. I felt happy, I was like "I'm going home!" But at the same time, in my mind, this is the best opportunity, because when I get out there, you know, I'm going to see the weed again, you know, when you like to smoke weed and you like to drink and be around girls and have fun. I had a specific girl that I was with for a long time, so that was messing me up too.

THE WHOLE PROCESS

I did everything.

On a regular day basis, I liked to smoke weed. I liked to talk to girls. I was around a bad company, guys that had a lot of girls and a lot of weed. I used to like the streets. I used to love the streets. I used to love gangbanging and stuff, everything – the whole process. I started cutting school. When you smoke weed, your brain cells die out and you get lazy. Every day, I would get dressed up and get ready to go to school, but by the time I'd hit the bus stop, it's like I'm too lazy to go through a whole process to go to school, so I turned back around like, "Naw, I'm not going to school, I'm going to chill at my boy's house." My mind was telling me to go chill with my boys, but at the same time it's telling me to go to school. I used to battle this and that, battle out, you know, I was in the gang at the same time, too. Hanging out with my boys, that's when I started getting knocked up and getting real records and stuff, real high and real records.

I would gangbang. I did everything: I gangbanged, I sold drugs, I held everything – guns. I did the violence. I fought for blocks. I robbed... I smoked. I drank. I was hanging with a whole bunch of girls. I did all that stuff, parties, I did everything. Now I feel like I'm too old school with it, you know, I don't need to do it no more, and it's not cool anyway. It was real stupid 'cause it wasn't for a smart course, like there wasn't no point of doing that. I realized how much education is important. Education and staying out of trouble.

Ain't nobody wanna be coming up here, you know, to see you in jail. Getting in trouble, you do anything wrong to people, it'll catch up with you later. You wanna go the wrong route, you gonna mess your whole life up. And as far as education, you can't get a decent job, you can't get a decent wife, a decent woman, you gonna have problems wherever you go. Like, say you gotta go to the supermarket and you're looking for a certain chicken – you gotta read, know what I'm sayin'? And you might go to a sneaker store, buy sneakers or clothes for a date or whatnot, so you want to buy certain clothes and you go to the store and they gyp you off. You know the price, but they gyp you off. You gotta know your math. It's the only way you're going to get through life.

Basically, what I'm trying to say is, it's always good to learn. If you don't learn, you're going to go the wrong path, that's it. You ain't going to get nowhere in life. If you don't know how to read, you can't get a job. You don't know how to do math, you can't get certain jobs, depending on what you want.

HARDCORE

I'm at that age where you start doing a lot thinking. My goal is to become a businessman. I wanna open up a gym. I developed that thought in a bad environment – I went upstate and I started working out, so I got cut up. I came home cut up, and I was like, "Damn, I should open a gym." When I came home I sat down and spoke to my boys about opening a gym and we all agreed to stick together and try to open a gym. If I could just get a associates degree, go to a good college, I could own my own gym someday. Mainly I wanna open up my own gym so when everybody is finished working out at my gym I could stay in my gym all day long and work out by myself.

I want a gym where you can lift some real heavy weights, but you gotta work hard. It's a hardcore gym, you can't come there and just do a couple of workouts. I wanna put up a sign saying it's a hardcore gym. I like to stay in shape. I like to keep my body looking hardcore.

In order to get in shape you have to follow the procedures. You gotta eat protein food – protein gets you cut up, gets you strong, gives you a lot of energy. You have to eat heavy food, you gotta drink a lot of water. You gotta take a lot of vitamin E because as you work out, it doesn't make sense to get your arms, your chest, your stomach all cut up and your skin doesn't look right. You need some vitamin E to keep your skin looking nice at the same time. I know how to work out.

When I went upstate, I was around a lot of guys that

have a lot of time – they've been up there for nearly fifteen years, so they're cut up. They been working out for a lot of years. They do it every day of their life. When I was upstate I would go to school, then workout, then go to program. You can't be lazy. There are certain things you can't do if you going to be in the workout process.

One day I was out in the yard and I seen this guy. He was in shape, his body looked unique. His arms was big, his chest was big, his stomach was cut up, his legs, his thighs – everything was lookin' right, for the girls. I said to myself "Damn man, maybe I could take advantage of this opportunity." So I went up to him and asked how you do arms, get your arms big? "Alright, you gotta eat a lot of protein and everything, you gotta do it five times a week and take a break twice a week to make your muscles heal, 'cause if you keep doing it every day, your muscles get tighter." He basically broke down the procedures for me and then I started working out. It felt good because I knew how to do it and I got used to it.

I spoke to him a couple of times 'cause we had something in common – work out – and that's when I started telling him about how when I get out I wanna open up gym, but I felt a little down because I didn't even have my G.E.D. so I felt like I'm not gonna get anywhere. I said to him, "I'm going to come home, I'm going to go to school and get my G.E.D. Then I'm gonna go to college and major in business, see if I can open up a big gym and put people in good shape, have people get their body correct." He said to go ahead. He gave me an address for a gym to go to in Harlem. I haven't heard from him, he's in another jail. I haven't worked out in so long, though, I fell off. I've been locked up here. I'm in school, I'm trying to get my G.E.D., I'm trying to accomplish this goal that I've had for so long.

THE IMPORTANT THING

This is the best experience I ever had. I never been around intelligent people. I don't consider myself intelligent, yet. The most important thing is to be smart. Somebody who's smart... you can recognize it when you talk to them. Like, for instance, I want to be like Mr. Rivera, my English teacher. He's so smart. I want a nice wife like him. I want to handle my responsibilities – that's what makes a good man. I wanna live a good life. I want to be intelligent.

I'm gonna be honest. I'm going to feel intelligent when I finish with this book – I never wrote a book before. I mean, can you imagine the first time you write a book? And you're young? That's unusual! You don't see a lot of young kids in my generation writing books like this. So, it's a good experience.

I want to write this book.

The Blue Print

Sam D

My name is Samuel D. I was born on March 21, 1986 in Brooklyn. Kings County Hospital, New York. Now I live in Queens. The earliest memory that I have about someone who taught me is my grandmother. She lived in the West Indies and I would go with my parents to the West Indies to visit her. She taught me lot. She taught me how to read properly she taught me every night how to read my bible and told me to keep praying and to go to church every Sunday. She would read a chapter in her bible and after that I had to read it back to her. Then she would explain it to me, about, what's going on. Every Monday's bible study and I'd go with her, you know. My grandmother also told me what her past was like, when she went to school, how school was like, back in the days. In school, back in the days you had to focus and stuff and there was no cutting class. She told me that she had to participate in class because if you didn't you'd be seen as bad and the teachers would call your parents. When you got home you got a beating. At least it sounded like that back in her days. Now, these days you get suspended!

My mother and my father, uncles, aunts, also taught me a lot. They always said stay in school get that education 'cause this world we living into you got to have something! You can't be lost all your time. You have to have some sort of education. You've got to learn something or you won't get anywhere.

My aunt, a teacher, also taught me a lot about school because there are kids younger than me. They know a lot! You know, they learn faster down there than over here. They learn faster because when they go home there's no watching no T.V. just get to your schoolwork and study.

My mother also taught me a lot and because I'm in here, she comes every visit. Every visiting day she comes, she wants see how her son doing. When I was young, when I was going to school she used to help me a lot with homework. My mom was always there, you know. She was always there for me. She was up to date with things. She wanted to know what's going on with me and, even now she is always coming up to visit me to see if I'm OK. Whatever my mom says to do I do because I respect her. I always do the chores like, or when it's when it's time to come in, I come in. I help her cook things like cake, um, rice and peas, oxtail, curry chicken or all that.

My role models are my mom and my grandmother and my aunt because they raised me right and, they raised me right to have a better understanding and knowledge. They raised me to learn more because nobody in the world ever stops learning.

My father, construction worker, also taught me about construction. I remember when I was nine or ten years old, I would always go to work with him. So I know I got an experience in construction. For example, breaking' down walls, plumbing, electrician, masonry, all that! I got experience in all that and, I know how to do all that. I know a lot about construction. My dad was a contractor and he had his own business, a construction company named after him. He's been doing this for twenty years. When he was younger he was a mechanic, then a taxi driver, then contractor.

When I was younger I liked working with my hands to try figuring out how to fix stuff. I sometimes used to get toys and I'd take them apart in order to see and figure out how they made it and how it would work.

I wasn't thinking of, being a doctor, a lawyer. Or, none of that, you know because construction came to my mind. Fixing things came to my mind and I'd stick to that. So I liked it because I'd remember things. I liked what I was doing and even so, to this day, I remember how everything went. A day that I went and told my daddy that I did something that I felt really good about was when I was younger I helped my dad fix the door. He was measuring a door. I remember I measured where the door was supposed to be. I measured the door and then drew a line and took a piece of wood to make a straight line so that my dad could cut it with the saw. I was also putting up walls!

Screwing up the walls with sheet rock. Sheet rock is paper–it's the paper wall. But in the middle there's like a chalky material which is easy to cut. You cut it with a knife or razor. I enjoyed it because it was fun especially because I always liked working with my hands.

I enjoyed seeing the door when it was put up. I'll say I felt proud. I was so young and somebody mentioned it, and said "Oh look how small he is; look how young he is!" They were telling my father that, you know, telling him to keep up the good work because one day he might have his son might have his own business in the future or something. I was young and I felt like I just won a million dollars or something. I was popular! Popular because every minute my name was coming out people's mouth, because they were saying, "He's learning something big and at a young age."

I was learning things and working with my hands so fast. I thought these people saying good things about me and it felt good in that way, man! My mom, dad, grandmother and aunt felt proud of me. I was young and I picked up, picked up something so good that, if I was to go like to a trade school or something people would say, man this kid got good experience and passion for something!

At this point when I was learning something big my friends were playing outside. Playing basketball and stuff and they couldn't believe that I could fix stuff. Yeah, 'cause they were into sports. I'm not really into sports like that but I'm into fixing things. You know, today I still work with my hands! As I got older, I got more experience, more different technology, became more open minded because I thinking that when I was younger, somebody that was my age back then wouldn't know about doing these things and I was working I started going to work with my posse since I was nine.

I also helped my mother and grandmother around the house fixing things. They were proud of me. I was fixing a lot of stuff. If anything went wrong, I'd take it apart. It might take me a couple hours, but I'd figure out the problem. I was also good at mechanic, too! I can change the oil of the car, change the oil of the breaks, the little fuse tips. Well, yeah, I am good at fixing things. I like working with my hands.

One thing that I wished I had learned more of was math because you need that every day. Everything that comes is math. I mean you need to do a lot of things in math. I know how to measure and all that, but I'm talking about twelfth-grade-math to college math. Since the thing that I want to do is work with my hands, I'm going to need math. I'm going to need it for estimating things and, and all that. For example if somebody gave me a job, I have to estimate the whole floor, estimate what it is I am charging them. I mean, you have to charge them with the material, plus how many days on the job. How much days it takes you to do it and you have to put all that together and make a, good price.

I learned and I know how to add, subtract, multiply, divide, but the bigger math, I get my head confused a little. I was learning it, I was just kinda getting it and I got it a little bit but, you know? I'd still mess up! I would get answers to problems then I'd go over and show the teacher and it would be wrong. Then I'd ask the teacher how to do it. He showed me how to do it. And I did it the right way. I came back up it was right! I feel good 'cause I went up and asked him.

When he was explaining why I didn't get it. Then I had to go back and work on the problems again and then he'd say it wrong again. The teacher explained in a better form back to me so that I would understand. I learned all this in high school. I had a good math teacher. In elementary school I also had a good math teacher. My dad was teaching me how to measure and I enjoyed it 'cause I was young and I was reading the tape measure, you know.

My favorite class in junior high was a shop class. We were making models of houses and I was making a lot of things, out of wood. I was doing ceramic too! I made a vase and I made a cup. I made a fruit bowl. It's in my house and it brings me memories.

I made a house though! I made a house out of foam. We had to use a metal twelve-inch ruler and a pen-knife to cut the foam. We also used glue to glue the walls. We used, wallpaper, and had, to get carpet and we used real carpet and toys appliances, like the refrigerator, the stove.

I made my house good. I took my time when I made my house. I was doing clean cuts. Everything was perfect, nothing was messed up, and I did good with my house. I passed that class too! I really liked that class. My stuff is still at home and, when I pass, I look at it and say, "Look what I did?" But the house that I made is still in the school because I told them that they can have it and keep it there for display. They might, use it and there might be somebody be in that class who will say "Oh that's a nice house! I wanna do something, and I wanna make something' like that!"

I remember the things and most of the things that I've made was back then, Junior High, in the nine/eighth grade. But I also liked the other subjects. People was jealous you know because their, houses came out sloppy and somebody in class was jealous 'cause I had a garage. I had the garage made into the house. I also made a porch, a step, and a door. I made two floors.

As soon as you opened the door on the first floor there was the, dining room. Then came the kitchen and two bedrooms on the first floor and two bedrooms on the second floor. There was a bathroom on the first floor and the second floor and a little attic. I had a fake fridge, a stove, a fake sink, a table, chairs, and real carpet on the floor. The wallpaper looked like, the wall was painted. I make it, I made the wall paint – it was a decorated. It took me, I think two months to finish because, I was neat and I was taking my time. I'm not a person that rushes. To put the house together you had to make clean cuts. So to put the house together and, in the middle is foam you have to cut it in an angle. You have to cut things so that everything fits together. Then you glue it with the hot glue gun because no other glue will work. I also had lights and, lights in there were like chandeliers which the teacher made.

Before we made the house we had to draw out a blueprint of how the house would look like. The teacher would give us magazines that had a lot houses so that you would have to flip through pages to choose one. The magazines had beautiful houses so I choose one I liked and then I made a blueprint. So the blueprint was how you want the measurements to be, a plan of where you wanted the rooms and how wide do you want them. Like putting out a plan, like, I wanted the garage, porch, dining room, bathroom, kitchen, etc. You have to measure the size and you have to put where you want the sink to be, the fridge. Well, we had to do that before we even started on getting the material together. It took me two weeks to do because I wasn't, sure how I wanted my house, where I wanted everything to be so, it took me a while to get everything organized.

When my mom came up for a parents-teachers conference, she couldn't believe, she couldn't believe her eyes when she saw my house. She said, she said, "You, you sure you did this?" Yeah, yeah I did this. Teacher said, "Yeah he did this." My mom was proud of me.

My dad didn't come up for the, parents-teachers. My mom was proud. While I'm here, in jail, I sometimes I go to my back, I think back and I say, "Look at all these things I did. Look at all these things I did in the past… and I'm in here. I say, I learned something and that I got a trade. When I get older

I've got something in my head that I know. And I am, not going out there now and know nothing. That's something. I have something in my mind that I know of. I know of a trade! And in life, you can't just sit back and think that things are going to come to you easy. Things don't come to people easy you have to work hard for it and you need to have a trade. Everybody needs to have a trade. Don't matter what kind of thing it is. What kind of subject or whatever it is, you need to have something.

I wish I could learn more. Learn a little more. Learn more of that, so that I can teach others, like, teach my mom, my sisters. I learned whatever they need help to always be there for my friends too and anybody else that really need the help. I don't have any problems helping nobody.

What I got on my mind and what I know in my head, in the future I might or probably, start a business or open a school a trade school for people on the streets or start a business like my own construction business. A trade would help them change their life around so that they can get work and leave the crime alone. Just open a little, a little center, for all ages. The younger people, when they get older, you know they have something on they mind to learn. I learned something that, nobody else will like. I learned a trade at an early age that I liked.

Gone But Not Forgotten

Biggz

My name is Biggz. I was born November 8, 1985 in Brooklyn, NY. I come from a large family. I got a lot of brothers, one sister—ten including myself. My oldest brother never grew up with us, so I am like the middle. So yeah, it's a big family.

IN THE WRONG FAMILY

The earliest memory I have was when my mother had my little sister. She went to the hospital and came back, like, three days later with a baby. My mother told me it was my sister, I didn't believe her. She didn't look like us. When she first came home she was real light, she actually looked like she was white! Over a period of time she started to develop features that look like the family, then I started to notice that her skin complexion started to change. She had started to fit in. You know like you see those movies where people get the wrong baby? That's what I actually thought, that my mom got the wrong baby. I asked her, said, "You sure you didn't get the wrong baby?" I didn't know what to think about her. I just asked my mother if she brought home the wrong people's baby 'cause somebody might be looking for her. And my mother just says, "Get outta here." She knew it was her baby. It kind of taught me a lot about how people, things change over a period of time. Now my sister looks like us, but at one point in time she didn't. She looked like she was in the wrong family.

THE PROBLEM SOLVER

I used to really ask a lot of questions. I was one of those kids that had to know everything. It got me in a lot of trouble and I would not stop 'til I got my answers. When I was younger there was a lot of things that didn't really have anything to do with me, but if it was happening in my house I felt I must know about it. Because of that right now me and my mother have this kinda special relationship where anything that is going on in my family I am the first to know. I consider myself as what you may call the problem solver. If someone has a problem in the family, they tell me about it and I figure out a plan to make the situation better. I've always had this kind of thing. I think it's like a gift. I've always had a plan for everything. Even as little kid I had a plan for everything. We lived on King's Highway, in Flatbush, in a basement apartment of a house. Once it rained, real bad, and the whole house kind of flooded. We didn't know what to do. We were gonna go somewhere else and stay and I said,

"You know? We can't do that. Let's pick the water up." But even if we took the water up, the water would still be in the carpet. I opened the door and let a lot of this water out and the rain stopped. Then I took the vacuum, plugged it in the wall, and sucked up the water. And it worked. I was about eight when this happened.

At one point in time my mother lost her job. I came up with a plan that if she didn't have no job then I would have to have a job. So I started to look about for places to work. I used to work in a supermarket, everywhere! I was twelve when I started packing bags in the supermarket. Every time somebody needed some help with something, I was there. I was very creative with things. Taking your bags to your house or car or even seeing people on the street that were carrying too many bags, I would help them too. They would give me a little tip, and I would just put it away. I basically spent most of the days in the summer looking for ways to make money. Everywhere there was money to be made, I was there too. Everything that you could possibly think of to make money, I tried. I was even sweeping barbershops and going on runs for some older people in the neighborhood. I did it all. It was just for the family. Doing all these little bits of work and putting away all the money, I actually saved a lot of money.

I learned that anything is possible. As long as you can put your mind to it, you can make anything happen. When I was younger I always knew what I wanted out of life and my mother always backed me one hundred percent. She's the one person that always kept me going. At the time a lot of people thought, "Ah, well, it's over for us." But it's not over—nothing is over unless you give up. And that's some thing I can't do. It was like throwing away everything that we worked very hard to build as a family. And I was never going to let that happen.

EVERYBODY'S FLAT TIRE

My mother is my inspiration. We have a one of the best relationships that a mother and son can have. She is a very intelligent woman. She's strong. All things most women want to be. My mother is my favorite cook. There is nothing she can't make. She taught me how to cook and it is something I love to do. Anything that can be made, she can make it. I like watching her cook. She makes her food with love. Most people just cook food 'cause they're hungry but she cooks sometimes just so other people can eat and enjoy. My favorite food is called chow mien. It's almost like Chinese food lo mien but it's homemade. My mother gets all the right ingredients like ginger, noodles, chicken and a lot of other stuff but when she's finished everything comes out perfect. I mean my mother won't settle for less than that. She is one of the most important people in my life and there are not a lot right now.

I had a father too. His name is Alvin. He was around but he wasn't around. I mean, my father didn't actually move away from me 'til I was about thirteen or fourteen. He didn't really play much of a big part of my life. I don't ever really remember my father doing very much for us. My mother had ten kids, and my father made eleven. She took care of him too. I never saw him actually do much, though he would fix stuff in the house. He taught me how to fix a flat tire. That was one thing about my father, he could fix anything. He was every kind of handyman—electrician, carpenter—so with that talent he had little jobs and stuff, but nothing permanent. He never contributed much to the family. And there was a lot of family. I remember when I was six or seven years old. My father lived on East 18th street in Flatbush. He lived in like a basement. In this basement they had a lot of bikes, old bikes, and he used to take them apart, put them together and build a whole new bike. And I had a bike that had a flat tire. He put on some glue and he had this leather patch. That's like the only thing I remember my father ever teaching me how to do. Since then, I've fixed hundreds! I've fixed everybody's flat tire. Hundreds.

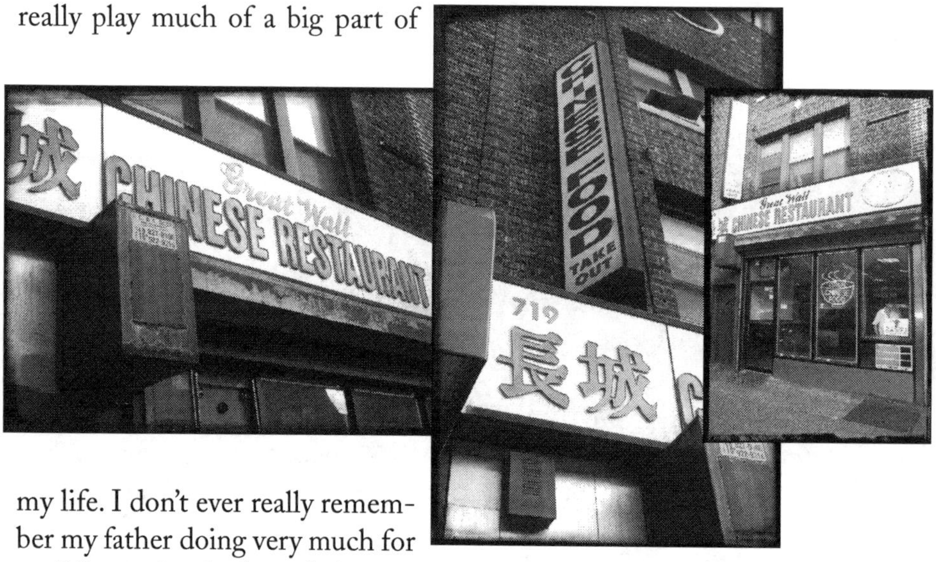

My mother was different. My mother used to have two jobs, and she went to school. She used to work in the World Trade Center. She used go through the numbers on a big chart, stocks and stuff that go up and go down. She would take it from that chart and put them on the computer. She would do this all night. Yeah, my mother worked hard. She had jobs that paid good 'cause we were always OK. She showed me that if there's anything that needs to be done, if you just put your mind to it, you could actually do anything. My mother is real strong. She's not really gonna fold. She's gonna stand strong. She's gonna fight the fight that she can fight until she can't fight no more.

BUT I KNOW YOU

I used to get in trouble a lot in school. Mainly because of my brothers. When we used to get in trouble we'd get in trouble as a group. It was like, everybody was going down together. And my mother used to be in the school every day. If it wasn't for me, it was for one of my brothers. I had this thing when I was young where, if you said something about me that wasn't true and I got in trouble for it, I then did it 'cause if I got in trouble for it, I was going to do it. I was in sixth grade at MS 2 in Brooklyn. I was in home economics class and I remember they called me to the office for something, so I'm walkin' by the door to go out. As soon as I stand by the door, the lights went off. I didn't think anything about it. I got to the office and everybody was like, "Oh, how I disrupted class. I turned out the lights, I was making noise in the dark." I didn't know what everybody was talking about! I just left the class! The principal was like, "Yeah, I'm gonna call your mother. I'm gonna have you suspended from class." I didn't even do anything! I got real mad and I called my mother. But after, when this was all finished, I went down the hall and down the stairs, back to the class, turned off the lights and left. I did it. I went back to the office 'cause they called my name again and they called my mother. I told my mother the first time, I never did it. She said, "But I know you and you said you didn't do it the first time but when you thought you were in trouble, you did it the second time." I said, "Yes I did." So she came to school, like she usually did, and had a conference about how bad I was. It was a conference to tell my mother how bad her kids were and, 'cause I had some cousins that went to the school, how bad her nieces and nephews were. So I mean, she was like, they can't be that bad. She fought with them for a long time.

VICTIM!

I left MS 2 because they finally kicked me out. They finally got the opportunity to get me when the principal one day decided that she was gonna curse me out. I had a very bad temper when I was young, very bad temper. The principal, she cursed me out, told me how I was stupid, how she didn't want me there. She was gonna suspend me. She called me to her office and was like, "You always causing problems in the school. I think you got a gang in this school." Ha ha, gang. I wasn't no gangbanger. She said I got a bunch of people that follow me. I had people who beat people up for me, all kinds of stuff she made up. She started going crazy. I never had anybody do anything for me I was gonna do myself.

I'd always be around people that did some crazy stuff. This all came about because there was this kid, right? A year younger than me. He was in fourth grade when I was in fifth grade. He was real big. His name was Jonathan. And, um, I don't know but for some reason everybody was scared of him because he was bigger than everybody. I mean, he used to sit in class and have his desk on his knees that's how big he was. I was in the schoolyard and my cousin was saying that she was in his class, my cousin Lahtia. She was like, well, he said so on and so forth about me, so I addressed him. He throw his big self up and I beat him up. He was my best friend after that.

Later on in junior high school, it was a bunch of us in the hallway by the auditorium and Jonathan had a sock in his hand and he put a pool ball inside the sock. He was just swinging the thing around. I said, "What you gonna do with it?" So this dude Matthew comes out of the auditorium and he was like, "Yo, let me see that." He took the pool ball inside the auditorium, hit this kid in his head screaming, "Victim!" and started running. He threw the pool ball aside and threw the whole sock back at Jonathan so we all started running in different directions. I went to my Spanish class and I'm sittin' there and the Spanish teacher asked me questions but I don't know what she's talking about 'cause my mind is gone. I'm out there. I'm thinking, "This kid is dead." They started calling our names on the loud speaker. I go to the office and the kid is in the office. He usually had glasses but his glasses is broken and he has a knot real big on his head. It's huge. The security guard says, "You come here, I know you did this." They said I hit him but they don't know what I hit him with. They took me, put me in this room and stripped me naked, lookin' for whatever they could.

PEGASUS WAS PUNISHMENT

Pegasus was the school where, I don't know how true it is, but years ago they threw the principal off the roof of the school building. It's true because when I actually got to the school, they confirmed it. The students threw the principle off the roof, but the roof is not actually that high. It's not two floors high. You could probably jump. And they didn't actually throw him off the roof. He was on a ladder and they say that they pushed the ladder down. So he wasn't on the roof and they just pushed him off, they pushed the ladder and he fell. It was kids being kids, kids being crazy 'cause they said the school was made up of kids that weren't wanted in any other school.

Pegasus was punishment. If you ever made it there, it was the last stop. You would never be anything in life. You couldn't do anything with yourself because you were going to school where they wouldn't teach you anything. It was like jail. Hearing all this stuff about Pegasus, I wasn't going nowhere next to that place. I was like, you thought I was bad? These kids were the devil and you sending me there? I'd rather not. But, later on, I found that not to be true. I went to that school. Actually, that's where I graduated junior high school from. I went to this school, it was like the first day, and it was kind of funny. I went in the classroom and there's only three people in the class, two students and a teacher. I'm sayin' to myself, "This whole school consists of three people?" I met the principal who said there's usually more people. This one that I was in only had two people 'cause some kids were out that day.

The first day I was there, I thought this place was crazy. There was this girl named Faith. She looked like a guy. She was bigger than me! I guess class was finished 'cause the teacher left and we was supposed to go next door to the other class. Faith grabbed this kid by his throat, threw him against the wall, beat him up, stripped him butt naked, and threw his clothes in the girls' bathroom so he couldn't get it. I'd never saw nothing like this in my whole life. The kid was completely naked, in the hallway, in front of everybody. She threw his clothes in the bathroom and then went to her next class. And this girl is in every class I went to. This was in September. School had just started.

Pegasus was actually the best school I went to. I actually learned something at that school. I actually worked. Every other school I believe they just didn't want me in their class, so they kind of just passed me. They were like, "Let's get rid of this guy." I mean, I was actually picking it up but they didn't care. They just didn't want me around. Teachers was like, "Oh, he was in this class this year? Alright, make sure that doesn't happen next year. Make sure he passes." At first I thought I got over it, but then come to think about it, I think

I was deprived of a lot of stuff. I mean, I was creative. I liked music. I liked stuff like that. I always participated in stuff like that but after a while it was like they just didn't want me around. I felt like not being wanted was something that was never gonna happen to me. I mean, I had a large family and half the time I wondered if they even noticed me.

MISS COLLINS

In Pegasus, I met a teacher. Miss Collins. She was West Indian so we had something in common. I have family all over the place—Jamaica, Guyana, England, Trinidad—all over the place. Miss Collins started out to be a language arts teacher. That was her title. But we never let anybody else teach us. The only teacher that was allowed to come into the class was Miss Collins. She started teaching us everything. She was down to earth. She would actually help you. Other teachers would put all the work on the board, or give you some handout or whatever, and say, "Do this." Miss Collins actually assisted you, you know what I mean? Actually tried to get you to understand what you were doin'. Why would this help you? Why would you need to learn this? She helped me. She helped the whole class. It was a better learning experience than our other teachers. The other teachers, they knew the type of environment they were in and they really didn't want to be there. "Oh, do this, do that. I don't wanna hear anything from you."

Miss Collins made me actually wanna go to school. She actually made me wanna continue school. She made me wanna learn. She made me wanna know. She helped me open my mind. Like what happened before in the other school, you're in a whole different environment. Whatever's over there is over there. It's behind you now. Now, let's do something productive. If we're gonna work, let's work. If you need help, I'm here to help you. And because the class was small, the maximum we had was about twelve people, she would individually help everybody. She even started something where she came earlier in the morning so she could help you if you needed help. She seen that we wanted to do it. Teachers in other schools would tell the class, you don't wanna do the work? Fine. I'll put it on the board. I'll give you the handouts. You don't wanna do any work, I don't have to teach you. My job is done. The principal comes around here, my job is done. I could sit around here all day. And I looked at that like, if you don't wanna teach me, I don't wanna learn. It didn't help me. I believe, in a sense, it hurt me.

I had another teacher in this school [Horizon Academy], Miss Roy. She became like a Miss Collins. Miss Roy taught science, math, everything. There was a couple of teachers—Donovan, the math teacher—who helped me. They were actually the reason why I even came to this school.

THREE GIRLFRIENDS

I stopped going to high school 'cause I kinda got into a problem. Not necessarily with the teachers. I had like three girlfriends at the same time. I was dating one girl and I stopped dating her and started dating another girl. And in the middle, this other girl who knew them, you know, was tryin' to talk to me. I don't remember really feelin' her, but I didn't wanna turn her down. I was like, I'm gonna deal with three at the time. One day, we had like a show in the hallway. We put on a show for everybody. That's not me. All that loud and outrageous, that's not me. Number one. If you have a problem with me or a problem with somebody, you express that with that person. You don't need all of this. You're hyping up all of this. I mean, school didn't actually get started 'til about one o'clock 'cause of this whole drama. Everybody was waiting to see what happened. Nobody was going to class. Everybody wanted to see what would happen. All the girls in the school decide they're gonna say that I was trying to talk to them too. I don't even know these people. It became huge. I'm walkin' in the hall and this girl would say, "Oh you don't remember?" No, I don't remember you. I don't know you. It became something that wasn't needed to be. And everybody turned it on me. I was like, I'm never going back. Everybody blamed it all on me. It wasn't my fault. After that situation, I just left everybody alone. I left school alone. A lot of things happened in the space of one week.

THE PRINCES

I actually wanna go to school for small business management. I wanna learn how to manage a business. I wanna start my own business and learn how to manage money, you know. Hire people, pay people. That's just something I wanna learn to make sure no one is being shorted or nothing. I wanna start a food catering service. That was something I always wanted to do. The first thing I'm gonna do is go to school for food preparation and catering. That's the plan, do the G.E.D. and start to look into how to go to college for that. And when I'm finished with that, I'm just going to, I'm going to try to broaden my horizons. Try to get a little business going on. Hire a few people.

I have a girlfriend, Tracey. She is very important to me. She is also the mother of my two children. My first son, his name is Justin and he was the only reason for me to go home but since I've been in here, Justin got a new little brother. His name is Joshua. My mother calls them the Princes. I think that with me being in jail a lot has changed but Tracey still comes to see me and stuff so I guess it's OK. She can sometimes be very hard to deal with but I love her. I even think that I'm going to marry her, but I think that I might be too young to make that decision right now. But I really think that's going to happen. When I was on the street I think I treated her the worst and I feel that I was wrong, but she is still by my side. I used to leave her and go out with friends and she wouldn't know where I was gone for a long time and things like that. But she was still there for me even after my first son was born and I was still doing the same thing.

That's how I got in this situation now. I'm in jail and have a whole life that I'm missing. My sons are getting big and they might not even know who I am. My mother says she won't let that happen, but who knows? She's says that I might be gone, but I'm not forgotten. I will be home and this will all be a memory in my past. And I'll tell my sons, Justin and Joshua, the things that they should not do to ever end up in this place. I'm going home to be a good father.

I have a lot learn. Anything in life is a lesson. You gotta take every lesson, learn from every lesson. The things that happen in life, everything, always teach you something—good, bad or indifferent. Bad situations...at the end of it, you come through it. And if you don't, somebody else could always see what was wrong and try to rectify the situation so you don't have the same problems again. The main thing is you learn from everything, you take everything as a learning experience. That's what I try to do. And that's what I'll try to teach my sons to do. That, and how to change a bike tire. Two sons...that's a lot of bike tires!

Never Settle for Less

D-Wop

My name is D-Wop. I was born in 1985 in Brookdale Hospital, Brooklyn, New York. I grew up in the infamous neighborhood in East New York, called Cypress Hills Project, where people robbed a lot, and stole, stuff. I remember David Dinkins the mayor came there, and they were shooting at him off the roof. I was like, "Wow, this is a bad project right here." That's where I was born and raised. When I was little we used to play football a lot. Stuff like that. Basketball. Anything really… skelly. Skelly is where you make milk tops—you get the milk tops, and you put wax in them to make them a little heavier. Then you make a skelly court. There's boxes, like one, two, three. You pluck the tops of the boxes, like that. It's a fun game.

My grandmother was my role model. She graduated from high school; she went to college. My grandmother taught me to always have my education—to get my education, 'cause you can't do nothing without it. She worked in the court system. She just kept, she took care of us. She took care of her family. She even took us—she had five nieces and nephews. She even took them in and took care of them. So I admire stuff like that. She's a Black woman who never had a man around to help. A strong, Black woman! My mom, a single parent, also taught me the value of hard work. Always work and try to get your education, because there ain't nowhere you could go without it. That's about it! I remember my mother always telling me to never settle for less than your best. That means never sell yourself short. If I had a job and I had an education, just to give you an example, why would I take a job that's going to give me five dollars when I have my education I can be making twenty dollars, I guess. Never settle for less. My mom had to work to feed us. And my grandmother too. She raised about eight of us. She had eight grandkids. She raised her daughters—she'd keep our whole family together. Without her, there's no family. And she told me, she retired. It paid off. She didn't have to work no more in her life. Just sit back. They were strong Black women and I admire that. No men around. And they raised the boys like me to become a man.

My mother and my grandmother taught me how to survive with whatever I had and to work. They taught me this 'cause I guess that's what the projects do to you. Like, the people that came up before me, they probably settled for less and they never got their education. When I was young—this was like '90, '89—I had to be about four, I used to see crack vials everywhere. I was like, "Wow. Why is it like that?" I understand now. Never settle for less than your best. My step father told me to always try to have a hustle or else I'm not going to make money or something like that. He meant packing bags, selling drugs, even when I was a teenager. He never told me to sell drugs, but it's anything. Helping people, cleaning up snow, just anything that's gonna accumulate money, I guess.

The older guys who had to be about eighteen, nineteen years old that was around my way also taught me something. I started doing dirt when I was about thirteen, fourteen. These guys just told me always to go out. Go hard. Never slack. Anything you do, you just got to do it to the fullest, whether selling drugs on the street, robbing, education, anything you do, just do it to the fullest. That means goin' hard. A hundred percent all the time and never settle for less. Whatever you doin'. It's a good jewel. That's a good thing to remember. That's something that I tell myself.

An experience that taught me something was probably selling drugs. Selling drugs taught me a lot. Even though it's a bad thing, it taught me how to manage my money, how to take care of myself. You've got to save everything. Drug money don't last that long. So whatever you've got you've just got to make the best of it. And you can't be cheap with that kind of money. You've got to—anything the family asks you for you've got to give it to 'em. It felt good doing that at a young age. About taking care of your family, working hard. This made an impact on me 'cause it's all I knew, really. That's all we had. Even though, you know, it's the life you chose. Coming up where I'm coming from, this is all we got. When I started providing for myself, I was about fifteen. My mother was strung out—she was addicted to drugs. So, before that, when I was younger, I was about nine years old, I used to pack bags, I used to give her money. She'd buy up stuff for the house and stuff. So it was like that at a very young age

I wish I had learned, I think just to get my education fully. That's what I regret—not having a high school diploma. That's it. Aw, man. I loved school when I was in elementary. The subjects I liked were Social Studies and Language Arts, and that's it. I had a teacher in 5th grade who taught a lot of Black history, and that really interested me. Just the whole aura of it. No, it wasn't just Black History Month. It was Black history every day. We had tests on it every week and all. One lady I remember, Madam C.J. Walker. She was the first Black woman millionaire who became one from products. Hair products and stuff. It couldn't have been easy in them days and I admired that. That's what I admired about her. Like, how could you become a millionaire when it was real hard back then for us. I had two teachers that I really liked. I had a lady named Ms. Horton was my third grade teacher and my sixth grade teacher, Ms. Harris. They kind of cared more than a regular teacher. Like, at the time I was with my mother. My mother was going through a lot of things. So I wasn't coming to school. Things like that. And I guess they cared. They contacted my grandmother, and my grandmother took over. Teachers don't get involved like that no more. I felt embarrassed at first, but I understand now. I'm thankful for that. Well, when they contacted my grandmother when I was coming to school looking like anybody's child, I wasn't coming to school, like that. I was young. About eight or nine years old. They knew that wasn't right. I felt they paid more attention to me. By yelling at me a lot. I remember I cut school. And they really went hard at me when I cut school. Yeah. It ain't like that at all, they knew I was a bright kid. Yeah, it's a good thing.

I guess a lot of classmates admired me. I still got the same amount of girls. In elementary school I always had a girlfriend, even though I was kind of bummy. I always had a pretty girlfriend. This was very important 'cause, I guess, someone of my caliber wasn't supposed to be like that. I didn't have much, but I never let it get me down. I always had the most popular girl. I could just see that I wasn't supposed to have something like that. Other people, other kids were wearing Jordans, Timberlands. I wasn't wearing that stuff. I was kind of bummy, like I said. Yeah, I had clothes on my back but it wasn't the clothes I wanted. That everybody was wearing.

In elementary school, I had a couple of best friends. My friend Danny, we've been tight since about the third grade. My friend Danny, we were from the same project. He was from the same place like me-a neighborhood guy. And this is when I was living in another project, so me and him kind of similar. He had a house full of kids. Eight brothers, eight sisters, so we was going through the same things happening. Having to pack bags, wearing reject sneakers, so we related to each other. And I had another friend named Rayshawn. Rayshawn, on the other hand, he was from a middle class family. He was like from a more middle class community. His mother worked, he had a father. He could get anything he wanted, you know. They gave me the best of both worlds. I used to go to Rayshawn house, I'd feel like I was, you know, livin' good, and then I had to face reality and go back to the projects with my man Danny and pack bags after school. When I saw how Rayshawn lived I wish I had a family. My mother and my father wasn't like that. It made me kind of jealous. But I never showed it, you know. That's a deep emotion. You know, deep inside. I wasn't jealous of him, I was jealous that I didn't have that. And I felt I deserved it because I was a good kid. We were still friends just until I moved out here. We moved out the area.

When I graduated, that was real successful. Because I had missed a whole month of school that year, I didn't think I was going nowhere. And it was real, it was real bad when you got left back, when I was coming up. It wasn't a good feeling. So that was real success for me. My family were proud of me, of course everybody. I went to the prom that year. My mother came to my graduation, my aunts, my grandmother. I was very happy. I was proud of myself. It was just—felt good just to see family there. Something I did, I achieved, myself. More about why I think I wouldn't have made it. I was going through a lot that year. I moved upstate. I missed about a month of school, two months. And I just came back. I passed.

A difficulty that I had in school was probably not, probably not fitting in with the kids that I sat with at my table in the classroom. Because I was in a small class. It was just different kids. They didn't go through the struggles I went through. They were happy every day. They wasn't going through much. They'd go home, do they homework, get money, sneakers, whatever they wanted. I had to go home and go hustle, you know, if I wanted to eat. So, you know.

Those were the kids that had mothers and fathers and they got anything they wanted. A family was really important to kid coming up at that age - a stable family.

Junior high it got worse. It got worse when I went junior high. That's when I started selling drugs. See, in New York, kids take on responsibility early. About fourteen, fifteen you're a grown man. You're not grown legally, but you're grown, doin' grown man things. My family at this point was still in Cypress. I was living with my aunt, then, I think. She was in East New York. It was very, that's very bad, out there. It's not even the kids that can choose to do this, it just happens. You're growing up. Kids bring guns to school. It was real crazy. I was into basketball then. I used to play basketball at the community center. Sixth grade, too. After seventh grade I started—that's when kids started breakin' their virginity. Stuff like that. It was 'cause we were just getting older. That's just what it is. I was very stressed out at a young age and that's no good for a kid thirteen fourteen years old. It was just a bad year. My mother was strung out on drugs. She didn't really care about what I was doin' in school. I used to cut school every day. I always dressed bummy. It wasn't like elementary school when I used to get girls anyway. It was different. You had to step your game up in junior high. I had some stepbrothers. Three stepbrothers. And I have a little brother. During junior high. They was around. They gave me a lot of advice and I admire them too. They schooled me on a lot of things. They taught me a lot about sports. They used to give me clothes. So I admire them a lot.

When I was going to little junior high school, I was going to I.S 166 A.K.A Garsh and then I went to I.S 218 A.K.A the 18, we ain't do nothing in school. It was just a shame. I was like, "Wow, this can't be life right here." Like, nobody was doing nothing. Everybody was just throwing paper, talking. The teacher don't even care. He's sitting back doing nothing. I was just like, "Wow." And that's when I figured, the teachers don't care. They getting paid, regardless. It's us that's losing out. That taught me a lot. That, you can't… like kids in other countries they would die to be where we're at - to get an education. And we're over here playing around with it. I made that connection because when I got older and looked back, I was like, "Wow, I wasted a lot of time." I could've been doing a lot with school. This was in Junior High. I stopped going to school after eighth grade because I felt that the teachers wasn't caring no more. I didn't care no more about school, I was like "This ain't going to do nothing for me." Naah. That's a lame excuse. I didn't care about school no more, it didn't interest me. I wasn't interested, I was bored. Everybody, you know, bringing money to school, kids my age, bringing guns to school. I guess that excited me, I liked it.

A learning experience that has shaped who I am, shaped my life is just the stuff I saw in life, I guess. Just everything I've been through, I guess. I don't know, really. The hood messes you up, man. Not really. It's very hard out there. The hood ain't going nowhere. It ain't same people, it's just… It's a treadmill, it's part of the circle. There are kids younger than me, coming up, you know. That's what I've learned, the hood ain't goin' nowhere never. The hood make you stronger, but in my case, and a lot of guys my age who—material things is what we want, we have to take away the hood. But the hood—I guess everybody wants to get out, and the only way you know how to get out is probably through sports, drugs, entertainment. After you don't want to play basketball no more, it's drugs. People from the neighborhood's lazy. You go to school—I dropped out of school, I'm sorry. This is embarrassing to say. After eighth grade I stopped going to school.

What am I learning now at this point of my life? That jail, aw man… Jail ain't where it's at. You need an education. You've got to take care of family. That's the only ones that's gonna be there for you in the long run. I want this education. I want it bad. I want it really bad. That would just give me the boost right now. That would up your self-esteem about the world, you know. You got a piece of paper. For real. I feel that I still have left to learn. Just on life experiences. Like, I saw a lot.

There's always—you never can learn enough. Just on life. I'm twenty years old. I'm young. Very young. I just got out of my teenage years. So there's always a lot to learn. One thing I'd love to learn? How to get rich quick, because I might have a chance of getting rich legally. Having an education, you know, open my mind more. And, you know, I do it then. One thing I have learned through my life experiences that I would teach someone else, is don't be a follower. Have your own mind. Go to school. And try to do something positive. You see guys driving nice cars, you know, nice clothes, it ain't all what it seem. There's a lot that comes with it. And a lot of people want to follow that. Just materialism. Material things. That's all they see in them. I'm saying... It ain't easy selling drugs, man. There's a lot of stuff that comes—your life is on the line. Your family's life is on the line. You're risking yourself going to jail.

You might have a family, you know? It ain't easy. Anything that got something to do with money ain't easy. I learned that, too. Like, trying to get money, you've got to work hard at it. Whatever you're doing, whether it's being a teacher, selling t-shirts on the street. Out there every day, every time. Consistent. And you got it. Yeah. Everybody's seeing you every day. Knowing you there. So right here. Being on time and consistent. Working hard.

If I were a millionaire today, I'd build recreation centers. I'd just do a lot of stuff for the neighborhood like fundraisers, football teams, all kinds of stuff. After-school programs. Just to keep the neighborhood kids. Keep them busy and keep them off the streets so that they never settle for less.

It's Like a Little Fever

Rico

I JUST REMEMBER LITTLE THINGS

My name is Rico. I was born in Lincoln Hospital in the Bronx. '86. March 11th, 1986. I don't know where I was living the first couple years of my life. But I think my mother was living—I think her and my father was living together in either a furnished room or an apartment. But I'm not sure. But I lived in the Bronx most of my whole life. I used to like school. When I was young, I liked school a lot. It was like, if I didn't go to school I thought I was going to miss something. I would go to school to learn and joke around. I was always real bright. The teacher would see me not doing nothing, and she'd be like, "Oh, what are you doing? Duhduhduhduh," like trying to scheme at me or whatever. Like I ain't learning nothing. But the teachers would be like, "You're so intelligent, you're letting it go to waste." And I'd be like, "I'm learning, you know? It's just that I don't got to sit here and be all glued onto you. I hear what you say. I'm learning from what you're saying."

It was just fun. School was just fun. I didn't like not going to school. School was just where everything was at. The friends is there, the girls is there, you know? I'm talking about young. This is young. I'm talking about like fourth grade.

My mother would be like, "Oh, you've got to go over here today," and I'd be like "No! I want to go to school." You couldn't get me to stay out of school. Word. For real. I would not stay out of school for nothing. Everything was just going on at school. You know, learning, too. It was—school was everything back then.

I remember being, whoooo, I was like…third grade. Second or third grade. I remember we had to write about somebody. We had to write about somebody, and I picked Nelson Mandela. I was going to the library. Doing everything for this one project. I know I was real young, too. Going to the library, looking stuff up about him, writing this report. Doing it over, and over, you know? Taking all this information and throwing it into one big story. For real.

That's the only project I went out for. Other stuff, I gave just enough. I don't know, I think it was like my first project and I wanted to prove that I could do it. I wanted to show people—and I wanted them to be like, "Oh look, you did real good on it!"

So mine's got hung up with like, three other kids', too. My report got hung up!

THE START OF A FEVER

You know how some guys, they used to hang out outside? I didn't start hanging out until I was, like, thirteen. My mother used to always be the one like, "You got an hour to be outside," and I had to be back after an hour. And I better be comin' back at nine-thirty on the dot, or, whatever time she'd send me out there.

If I didn't I would get beat up! For real. I would just hear her mouth, and that's the worst, because she would be screaming all these things. She used to only—sometimes she would give me two hours, three hours. She didn't want me to be outside. She just didn't like me being outside. She used to feel like, you know what I mean, there's too much stuff going on out there.

Once I was like, twelve, the streets started hitting me hard. I couldn't get enough of the streets, kid. I used to—I'd leave, and I'd go outside, knowing that she's going to be very upset by the time I come home, so I'd just be like "Yo, instead of coming an hour late, she's still going to scream on me, so I might as well come a couple of hours late," you know? Like, for real. She'll tell me—she'll let me out like around four, and she'll be like, "Come back by six," you know... When it starts getting dark.

I'd already be like an hour late. It'd be like seven, seven-thirty. Shit, I'd just be like "Yo, she's going to scream on me anyway, I might as well just say I

lost track of time and stay out here until nine, ten, till everybody goes upstairs," you know?

For real. It was like a little fever. And then I started being in the streets with my peoples, you know. We was doing different things, there was stuff we wanted. Once I started getting a little bit of money, it was a wrap. Streets grabbed onto me. It was hook and sinker. I didn't want to do nothing. For real.

High school was fun. I was like the flyest dude in my—I can honestly say—in my school. You know? I would go, and I'd be fly and all that. Have whatever was new was on me – at that time it was these Coogi sweaters. You know, a pair of Vasquez boots. A pair of jeans and stuff. I'd go to school just fly. And all the girls is like, "Ohhh."

I'm young, I got a little money in my pocket. I'm like, fourteen, dressing like—you know a sweater cost four. Boots cost two hundred. I'm fourteen years old, you know? Word. I was getting high.

Let's say—I'm a person—I can't smoke early in the morning or nothing like that, because then I won't get nothing accomplished that day. If I go, let's say I'm about to go to school, right? I go stop by the store and cop me a sandwich or something. And if I smoke me some weed, I ain't going to wind up going to school that day. Because I'll be so high, and I'll be looking like—and I'll just be feeling like such a loser. I'd be like, "Yo, all these guys is going to school and I'm just sitting here getting high." I'm thirteen, fourteen years old. I'm taking cabs back and forth to school.

By the time I was fourteen I already had a '91 Honda. Fourteen years old! I'm parking around the school. Guys is like, "Yo we gonna ride the train together?" and I'm telling girls, "Yo, we could go in the car." What am I doing? I'm fourteen years old.

TONY MONTANA

Alright. My role models, since I was young, I could say was like my stepfather. In the beginning. Then, once I started hitting the streets I just started looking up to these two older guys. Once I got a little older, I like "These older guys ain't really doing nothing." I started looking up to other people. Characters in movies and stuff like that. Those would be my role models.

Scarface. You know the kind of movie I'm talking about. Al Pacino, yeah, Scarface. Yeah, that character. Tony Montana. And Manolo, his trusty side-kick. He went from not having nothing to just having everything. I don't know. When I was younger, right? And kids go around, you know, I was like in fifth grade and this memory really sticks out a lot…Teachers be going around to kids, asking kids what they want to be, right? And I'm sitting there, in my head, I'm like "I'm going to tell her something." But I know in my head, "I want to be the man." You know what I mean? "I want to be the guy that's in the street, getting money," you know? That's what—I just always wanted to be that n____ getting money. For real.

I didn't want to be no police officer, no fireman. When I was little I wanted to be a cop when I was younger, but once I got older I was like "I don't want to be no cop!" I want to have that car. I want to have that big chain. I want to have this. I want to have anything I want." Like that?

That's a memory that sticks out. What kind of kid at that age is thinking about being in the streets and getting money? I mean, this is like fourth, fifth grade. Fifth grade, at the most.

My teacher, she say, she was just like, "Anything you say is confidential." I forget what I told… I told her some stupid shit, probably like plumber or something. I was like "Yeah, I'm gonna be a plumber." But think about it, a kid who sees somebody like my stepfather. I saw my stepfather work hard. Every day. You know, like as far as the house and everything. Everything you had, you know, it makes you really happy because you never wanted to be… you wanted to be average. Just providing for the family.

And he was providing for the family, and then you'd see these guys out there in the streets. They out there, they're driving this, they're driving that. They got all the women, you know what I mean?

They got the… brand new, everything was brand new. Everything that cost too much for a regular working person to pay for, you know. A person who works—it's a week or two worth of work. And he has that on his back! "Oh, this is a couple of hours for me."

Yeah, when I was young my stepfather always had his little cars, he had motorcycles. He worked hard. He had a lot of hard work to do. He'd come home, tired. All he wanted to do was watch a little T.V., you know, and go to sleep, you know.

I'm seeing these guys on the block, they on the block all day! They've got the same stuff he got, even more. All it look to me like is the were hanging out, that's what it looked like, like they just hanging out, when in actuality, they out there on the paper chase....

Who you think I'm going to look up to? I'm a person. Like I said, I like having everything that's—I like to shine outta the whole crew, it's like... Me, I'm materialistic. Caught up... in the glitter of everything.

JUMPING OVER THE GATE

When I was like probably fifteen, sixteen, and I caught a little D.F.I. bid, I was doin' a little D.F.I. time... I wanted to do good and all that. I was in a good school before I went to D.F.I. You know, I got trialed... I got sentenced to eighteen months.

I was supposed to go up in these mountains for a couple of months, have like a year outta my life and then come back home.

What wound up happening was I ended up staying in Trion for a year, and then stepped down for another two months. Right there, that's fourteen months! I probably had a little, like four month outside on after-care, and I just kept on violating that.

At the beginning, I first came home, I didn't want to smoke weed, I didn't want to drink liquor. I didn't want to do nothing. I wanted to get me a job and go to school. As soon as I start trying to get into school, my old school doesn't want to accept me. They're talking about, "Oh, you had problems. We want to see him go to school for a couple of months at a different school, and all that. Before we take him back."

So they sent me to some school that's not for a person who wants to get focused—to go to. I'm easily distracted. I'm going to school and I'm just feeling like a regular dude, and I'm just like—like let's say somebody just thought they was rich, and then outta nowhere they feel like they poor again. And none of these guys is sitting that they doin' it. You know what I mean?

You know what I mean, they think they're the most money-getting dudes that ever walked this earth, you know. I felt like a dinosaur, like "This ain't me right now," you know? I wasn't able to really focus on school. I started cutting—I never used to cut at school. I started just leaving. Like, ten o'clock, I leave. twelve o'clock, I leave. Jump over the gate, like... "I ain't stayin'." Cause it wasn't fun to me no more.

School used to be fun, right? Like, I'd take care of my work and all that, and I'd still chill out. I didn't know none of these guys, you know what I'm sayin'? In the Hills for like, almost... fourteen, fifteen months out of my life, I already got used to like a different setting and all that. I went to this school, I wasn't used to this.

Because I was so young and they took me out of my frame—out of my environment. You know you don't just stick a kid that's fifteen, sixteen years old… for petty stuff—you don't stick him in the Mountains for no year and change out his life. You don't do that. You know what I'm sayin'? Eighteen months. That's a year-and-a-half right there. Kid's fifteen years old. What are you doing?

It was like, I'm looking around and I can't really get focused. Like this teacher is just talking, and I'm just standing there looking around. I just feel like I didn't fit in.

I felt weird. I couldn't just get focused on it. I'm coming to school, and you know, dudes is just like… lookin' at me like "Who's this guy?" You know what I'm sayin'?

But you gotta understand that. It's like, these dudes is already like, in their second, third grade. I mean in their second, third year of that same school. I'm a new dude, I'm coming in like… That didn't feel right. I didn't even live on that side of town, so it's like I'm in a whole different side of town with nobody I know. I said I was kind of cocky, so if I don't know you I wasn't trying to get to know you.

PAPER CHASE

I went to the streets! To run the streets and get money. That was my whole—it was like a game. That's how fun it was, it was like a big game. Yo. I wouldn't even really hang out—I didn't do nothing besides go out there and get money. That's all I used to do, all day, every day. It's a paper chase, kid. It's like it never ends, it's like "Yo, I have this and I have that," but it won't be enough. It got to the point when a person got a couple of hundred in they pocket and it's still not enough, like, come on, I'm broke right now. Dudes is lookin' at you like "What's wrong with you, you turning greedy, kid." I'm like, "It's not enough." For real.

It's worse than a job. It's worse. It's worse than a job. That's all, like, a person does. Wake up, brush your teeth, and you take a shower. And they throw on their clothes or whatever. And they go outside and they just do what they do. You get what I'm sayin'?

After you finish that, go upstairs, you know, smoke a little weed or whatever, take a shower and go to sleep. And you got to give a little, to the girl who's there that you're living with. You know. Hang out with them for a while. Go to sleep.

The first thing you've got is a ringing phone early in the morning. "Yo?" "Yo." "Rico, I need this, that, alright," you know. Go, take a shower, brush my teeth, and come outside. Once I'm out there it's a wrap. I'm staying out there until I reach my quota, you know what I'm sayin'?

It got to a point where not only am I gaining more money, but I'm spending more money too. Just to get by in a day a person is spending a hundred, a hundred and fifty dollars. That's just on weed and food. Anybody—these guys that's out here on a paper chase, they're going to agree. They all know it's true. We don't be setting no goals for what we're doing this for. We just do it to do it. That's just what it is. That's just like a big game. It's like a big game.

At the end of the day we'll see our profits or whatever. But at the end of the week you don't see you no profits, we done blew it on jewelry, on cars, on this... You look at it, you don't be having nothin'. I know I've got this amount of money because I go out and buy gold earrings. When you need money you pay twelve hundred for them, they only givin' you two, three hundred for them. If you're dropping thirty-two on a chain, they only going to give you a thousand dollars, if that, at the pawnshop.

Actually, a legal job is you do your eight hours and you're gone. This is all day. It's on-going. You go to sleep thinking about money, you wake up thinking about money. That's all it is. It's a big paper chase. I'm out there, you've got to work it—you've got whatever it is you're doing when you're outside. It's a fashion show out there, so you out there tryin' to be the flyest dude on the block, whatever, you know what I'm sayin'? You've got the females coming through—they're purpose is, they're just coming through to try to grab the attention of the guy that's getting money. That's they whole purpose. They dress up, or whatever, just to grab our attention. That's what that's for. We're out there just to show them who's wearing the most money out there.

Usually I might have a—"I've got this kind of chain" and "I've got this kind of chain." "I'm getting the most money out here, you understand?" It's a big fashion show. It's crazy. And then you see the people that's getting their drugs, walking up and down the block, and there's a whole bunch of activity going on. There's a whole bunch of stuff going on. And if you don't know—like everybody's playing a role in this. Everybody's playing a certain role. For real. You need to be just so fast, everything's just so fast-paced—you don't even have a second to just take a breath and be like, "Yo… this wasn't supposed to be goin' down like this." But you don't be thinking that. You just thinking "I'm out of here, I've got to try to finish this so I can get the next one." For real.

Tougher in the streets, yeah! And like I said, it's not a job, it's an ongoing thing. It's all day every day. "What you doin?" "Getting money." Even if I go out to the club, or whatever. Like I party and stuff. Soon as I leave the club, the first thing I think is "Damn. I just spent 800, 1200." Whatever it is, you have to hit the block… make that 1200 back. Whatever it is, make that back. It's crazy.

I think about, I never used to do nothing, I wouldn't hang out or nothing, 'cause If I'm outside, I'm tryin' to make money. Just getting money all day.

YOUR OWN SPOT

Ah man… I had a whole bunch of dudes—when you can say you've got your own block, or you got your own spot or whatever, you've got dudes coming at your throat all the time, man. All the time. Somebody owe you, you've always got to throw your point out there. So, it be… little old me, I'm only a hundred and forty, a hundred and fifty pounds. I'm five-something. You know what I mean? Skinny. I'm out here fighting a dude that's six-foot something. You know, his weight class and everything is higher than me. And I'm out there fighting, trying to get the best of him, too. For real. Just trying to prove my point out there. It used to be crazy.

There'd be dudes. You'd be out there. There'd be a dude out here, he'll take something little and make it mad big because he's wanting to prove a point to everybody. So every time you'd be like, you doing stuff to everybody else. 'Cause they watching. For real. You don't be doin' stuff for yourself, you doin' it for every body else. For the crowd.

Not only that, you getting money, you want to keep your position. You don't want to lose your position; you want to gain in your position. You want to get more… you wanna own more stuff. You want to be the boss of more places. You don't want to be a boss and then become a worker.With me, this guy—my man now. He was my friend from juvenile, know what I'm sayin'? Me and him bumped heads, because we're out there, we on the strip, and we're doing whatever we do out there. And we bump heads real quick. We had a little argument or whatever. So me and him exchanged words, and he left.

So a couple of days later, I'm talkin' with my moms, he disrespected my moms or whatever. So, I went in… you know… grabbed… you know… stuff out my closet and stuff… I came outside... So I asked him, I'm like "Yo, you disrespectin' my moms?" And he just came chargin' at me. I just tried to… I tried to end this guy, you know what I'm sayin'. Luckily… in the joint… I had problems, you know what I'm sayin'? I didn't get to do nothing. But I wound up hittin' this dude repeatedly, you know what I'm sayin'? So, he came back and he chasin' me, he lookin' for me with a gun. So all day, let's say I go to the block. If he's not out there before I'm out there, then he's not going to be able to come outside. Because as soon as he comes outside it's going to go down. He's not going to come out the building without me knowing he's about to come out the building, and I'm gonna go do what I'm tryin' to do.

And I know, do whatever I do, this guy is trying to kill me. And it seemed like, vice versa, if he's out the building, I know as soon… I can't come out because he might start shooting. So I don't even want to step outside the building. So it was like an agreement thing. we both—I don't understand. It was an agreement thing – he'd be outside in the morning, I'd be outside at night. That's just how it was. He'd go upstairs, like, ten or eleven. I'd come outside at like eleven till probably nine at… nine, ten, eleven o'clock in the morning. Once I go upstairs, I eat, I go to sleep, wake up. Look out. He's out there, and I've got to fall back for a little while. He do the same thing. When we run paths, it's war. We do what we do, chasing each other up and down the block. It was very close. It got to the point where I'm like, "Wow. This guy lives in the building right next door to mine."

So we're bumping heads every day. Every day is a close call. Every day I'm ducking behind shit, you know, and it's the other way around. He was ducking inside buildings. He was a trying not to get hit.

KEEP ON 'TILL I GET IT

I be looking at my past sometimes, and I be like "Wow." The thing is, I used to go out there and do things. But I never really needed anything, it's 'cause I wanted stuff. Like. Boom. My mother would spend a hundred and something on a pair of Jordans, you know. She'd just be like, "Yo, you better not ask me for nothing for a little while," but I'm like, a pair of Jordans, or a pair of hundred-dollar boots. That wasn't enough for me when I was at a certain age. I'm like, "That's not enough. I want a couple of pair of hundred-dollar sneakers in the closet. Brand new. I could just throw 'em on. I could wear a pair of different sneakers every other day." Every day, you know? A different pair of boots, a different outfit. I just had to be in the spotlight. I couldn't feel like I was second. I had to be number one. I had to be, "Ohh…Rico got this, Rico got that." I always liked to be in the spotlight.

Like you got a pair of Jordans, I've got 'em in every color, though. Like that. I don't know. For real. I was confident about myself. You couldn't tell me nothing! Like, "What? Don't tell me nothing." You couldn't tell me nothing, for real. I was just a—as soon as a girl come through, and she's pretty? I'm the one who's trying to snatch it. And if I aim for it, I'm getting it, too. If I aim for her, I'm going to get her. I always was like that. I'd just go after them, chase them. I'd do the little games they want to play. For real. I always accomplished what I want, though. Word. When I set out to do something, I keep on 'till I get it.

Like let's say, for instance, besides girls, right? Let's say we're materialistic, then. Let's say, "I'ma get this"? I'ma get it. Let's say, for instance, "Oh, that hat" or, you know, little things. Sneakers or something. Or a coat. If I be like,

"I'm gonna get that," I'm going to get it! Trust me, I'm gonna get it. Once my mind is set, I'm gonna get it.

I used to tell myself, "Listen. I'ma keep on going to school. I'm going to graduate, at least I'm going to make it to at least tenth grade." Like this. I'ma keep on doing this. Yeah, if I try… If I set out to do something… I'ma try, I'ma get it. I'ma do it. And if I don't get it? Whooo, that's the worst man. For real. There was things I missed out of. I missed out on a normal lifestyle. See, at seventeen, I'm out here getting money. I'm getting whatever I want. Whatever's hot I want it. Whatever the rappers got, I want it. Whatever I see on T.V. that someone's got on, I want it. Know what I'm sayin'? And I've got to do better than that. He rock it like this, I've got to wear it like this. I've got to do it better than him. You know? For real. I've got to go down Fordham , I gotta see what's new.

It got to the point where I used to go down—where I'm at, is right there on Fordham.

No, like. You know how Fordham is, it's a very long trip. I used to walk all the way from University by the church all the way to the end, and I wouldn't see nothing that I ain't already had, or was worth buying. Like when I have whatever amount, I'd come for whatever. Whatever it is. I'd be walking down Fordham, and there don't be nothing that I see that I want to buy. I was like, "I already did that. This person already got it on the block." Or "That's not official enough."

I don't know, that's just how I always wanted to just do. That's how I just wanted to be like. If I set out to do this, then I wanna be able to do that. You know? I think it's from, like, not wanting to fail, right? Not wanting to fail.

After That, I Was Still Being Bad

Taimak

My name is Taimak. I was born in Lincoln Hospital in the Bronx in 1985, March 23rd.

The neighborhood I grew up in is kinda wild, a lot of shoot-outs, people selling drugs. I grew up right around that neighborhood. I was on 166th and Finley Avenue, a couple of blocks from the Grand Concourse. I had one little sister, Tiana, she passed away when she was two. She passed away in 1996. She was real sick. She was doing well when she was in her first year, when she was one year old. Then after a while, she got real sick and she had to be in the hospital. She had to be in the hospital for almost a year I think. I don't remember, I think it was pneumonia. But she passed away in the hospital. I was around eleven. It made me, like, stronger, I don't know... like whenever people is saying stuff about me, I don't really react to it. They call me a punk or anything, I won't really egg 'em on to it. I let things go a little bit. I have two older brothers on my father's side and my little brother on my mom's side. My little brother and my little sister had the same father. In pre-school, pre-kindergarten, there was this girl I knew who had a crush on me. Her name was Jessica and she was Puerto Rican. I was five. Every day I used to go to school, she's always teasing me and barbing and stuff and I was just like one of the quiet kids and um, one day I had a little birthday party and my mother had brought me a cake and she brought me to school so we had a little party for the whole class. I had the cake on the table, and the girl that had a crush on me comes in and digs into my cake and started messing up my cake,

cutting pieces out of it without the teacher's permission. So she kind of like ruined it up for me, and um, later on that day one of her friends that she used to hang out with had told me that she liked me. I still see her. She lives around my block now and she dated one of my friends. My friend passed away. He got shot. I was a bad student in middle school. I was very aggressive. I was a troublemaker. I was always starting trouble with people. Like, this one time, I was at class and there was a Dominican kid I used to know. He was doing his work. He used to always do his work. He was quiet, always do his work and I used to take a piece a paper and I'd throw it at him. So one time, I threw a piece of paper at him, he gets up and he taps me on my shoulder and says "Hey, what you doin' that for? Why you throwin' paper at me?" So I tapped him back, and he tapped me back harder, and I tapped him back harder. So then he hits me real hard in my chest and the teacher was like, "Stop, break it up, I'm going to talk to you after school." So after school I went up to him and I was like, "What's up now? You want to fight or something?" I went up to him and I punched him in his face.

We started fighting, fighting in front of my friend's house. Then after that, my other friends came and we jumped him. There were five of us. We jumped him and whatever, and we ran to my house 'cause we were scared that the cops were going to come. I was thirteen. I kind of felt sorry for the kid 'cause we jumped him. He didn't get a fair fight. But I didn't ask nobody to jump in, they jumped in themselves. I don't know, they thought I was losing so they had my back. He tried to get us suspended. He told the principal what happened. Next day I came to school, I almost got suspended. So I told the principal nothing really happened, it wasn't me, know what I mean? I didn't want to get in trouble. My father was like, if I get in trouble, you'll get a punishment for a long time. I got in trouble a lot in school. I got into a lot of fights. One friend's name is Toddy. His name is Todd but we called him Toddy sometimes. We always worked together, helped each other out with each other's work. He was like one of my best friends in junior high school. We'd always worked together, helped each other out with our works like math. I think that's why I'm so good at math, because we boys always did math together. We'd always talk about girls, what we'd do after school, there were times that me and him'd cut school. We play hooky. See in this house, there's like this abandoned apartment or whatever... nobody lives there. We used to go to the abandoned apartment and we'd all gang up, all my friends at school, we'd go up there and smoke weed and we'd chill, talk and we'd have some girls up there or whatever. There'd be like five boys and like four girls. We'd have fun, play around with each other and stuff. After that, we'd go get something to eat, go up to McDonalds or something. One time I came over there, I think it was around November. I know it was cold though, it was real cold. We went to this hooky party or whatever. These Spanish people, they put on a hooky party. It was right around my high school, Taft High School. It was a big party, loud music, people just throwin' it in the air, and stuff. Me and my friends, there was like three of us, we stood there for like four hours.

Hooky parties were like a regular party. Everybody cuts school and everybody meet up in this one area and stuff. Sometimes they would have music and food and you'd do whatever you like, like smoke weed, smoke cigarettes. Sometimes they'd be in an abandoned apartment, sometimes they'd be in someone's house like their parents would be at work so we'd go there.

Toddy's still one of my friends. I just saw him recently. He's in the same facility. I used to go to the yard every day to see him and stuff, you know, talk about what happened in the past. Like one time we met up in the yard and I was like, "Yo, what happened, yo? I just heard, you just got locked up?" "Oh yeah, you just got locked up too?" So before I got locked up I used to talk to this girl that he know too. I messed with this girl. And it just so happened that this girl I used to mess with, he used to mess with her too, but he live on a different block. So he's like, "Yo, this girl asked about you." And I'm like, "Word? She asked about me? What'd she say?" He's like, "Um, she's like that you got locked up or whatever." Does that mean that she miss me or something like that? So I'm like "Well, that's what's up." I don't talk to her no more. I talk to my girl. She's a better girl. I get more respect. This girl listens to me a lot. I like a girl that like to be around me that's faithful... That girl that me and him was talking about, she wasn't faithful.

Taft was, like, a bad school a little bit but also a good school. I could learn in that school. I could learn a lot of stuff there. It's kinda like a bad school too because there used to be a lot of fights there. One time, it was my first year of school in Taft, in ninth grade, I was in a classroom and I ain't know nobody. This kid was always like a class clown, always a clown in every class, and one time he was joking around in a class that I was in. So I was laughing at him. I was sitting down doing my work and he take a piece of paper and throw it at me, so I turned around. He started laughing, so I'm like, "Alright, you wanna throw a piece of paper?" Said to myself, alright. We had to change class and I met up with one of my friends whose name is Abassi. He's Jamaican. So I'm talking to my friend Abassi and I'm like "Yeah, this kid, he must think I'm, like, a punk or something. He threw a piece of paper at me." He said, "Point the kid out." So I point the kid out and Abassi went to the kid and was like "Yooo, you threw a piece of paper at my friend?" And the kid denied it so I'm like "Yo, he lyin', he lyin'" and I tell my friend Abassi. So my friend Abassi mushed him in the head. The kid looked back and my friend Abassi kicked him in his butt and he started running so he started chasing him around the hallway. And then the kid ran to the principal and Abassi ran out of school. The other kid got in trouble for running in the hallways. He tried to tell the principal what happened but the principal didn't believe him. He just saw him running in the hallways.

In the high school I wasn't a trouble-maker as I was in junior high school. I became more mature than I was. In high school I was more quiet, and in junior high school I was like one of the class clowns. I was always like class clowning, you know, joking around, loud all the time, the one person that always be loud. I used to always mess with the teachers. I liked to be loud, make funny noises, make everybody laugh. I did that because I would be bored. And you know, in junior high school I was in Special Ed. There was this one floor for Special Ed. I remember there was this one time in junior high school, I had a book laid out on the desk. I went to the bathroom and this kid, some Spanish kid wrote a curse word. I don't want to say the word but, um, "F your mother" on a book. So I came back, I saw it laid out on my book and I was like, "Yo," I sayin' out loud, "Who wrote this in my book? Want y'all to man up, who wrote this in my book?" So my friend Todd, remember my best friend Todd? He was there and he told me, "Yeah, yo, that kid, that Spanish kid named Joseph." So I go to this kid Joseph, "Yo, you wrote in my book?" "No, I didn't write in your book." He got up, "I didn't write in your book." I go, "Yo, I already know you wrote in my book, somebody just told me." "Yeah, I wrote in your book, whatcha gonna do? Yeah I wrote in your book." So I snuffed him. Punched him in his eye. After that, the teacher came all "Hey, hey, hey," 'cause this kid Joseph is rubbing his eyes and crying and stuff. So the teacher came, said "Hey, hey." I ran out of the classroom and I got in trouble 'cause the teacher told the principal what happened. The principal called my parents. My father came in and he was talking to the principal and the principal was telling my father what happened and my father, just, he slapped me. He's like, "Yo, you need to stay out of trouble man. If I keep coming to school you'll be on punishment for like a month." After that, I was still being bad. I had this habit of throwin' pencils....I mean, I would sit down, do work. I always got high grades even though I was a trouble-maker, yeah. When I went to high school they took me out of Special Ed.When I graduated out of junior high school, my mother, she caught a stroke. I can't remember what year it was. She was sick, so I had to move to Florida. I moved to Florida for one year. I lived with my grandmother for one year. And I had a situation with my grandmother. I was going to high school out there, the ninth grade. I got left back in ninth grade. When I came back to New York I was still in ninth grade. That's when I went to Taft. But what happened was, I was down there for a year and I was doing good too. I was offered a job. I had a girl that wanted to get married to me. I was age sixteen and she was two years older. I met a lot of people. I was popular. I was very popular. A lot of people liked me so they wanted to hang out with me. I would go to school out there, I was cool with the teachers. They always helped me with the work.

That's How I See It

P. Abdullah Stroman

All right, my name is P. Abdullah. I was born in Wilmington Delaware. I lived there for five years. Then I came to New York. To Brooklyn, in Bed-Stuy, Saratoga between Jefferson and Hancock. I was there for four years. Then I moved around. I went through—I went through a lot of trouble, going in and out of shelters. Stuff like that. Moved from the Bronx to Manhattan, from Manhattan to Queens, then I moved back to Brooklyn. And then to Queens again. I'm from the Queens borough, well—I'm from Brooklyn but I just live in Queens, that's what I say.

STRENGTH

Everybody is gonna be tested. I see it, when I'm home or walking down the street and you see someone, you know. He look like the violent type. Like they say, when you come upon things like that, you know, be the bigger man to walk away than to act on whatever is about to come towards you. We see it in here, many individuals, you know, they are testing your strength and your spirituality by saying something to you. A lot of individuals act off of verbal responses. That's how I see it.

I have to look for strengths in myself to be the better man, to not be the violent one—always be humble. When I say the better man, I mean not to be perfect, but just to know within yourself that you can do such and such with the situation; be the first one to change that around, not make the same mistake that he's about to make or the same choice or follow up the way he's about to do. You have to make the opposite decision, bein' the better man.

Honestly, because a lot men, they let their pride get in their way, or their ego. You have to, for me, to look deep inside myself, for my strength, I have to look past my ego and pride, you know. I have to fight with my ego and pride to not to do this and not do that, just telling myself, "Look man, you can do this, this is not worth it." Because in a lot of situations, you wind up... It's hard looking in within yourself. Looking for those strengths, but if you got a lot of confidence within yourself, it shouldn't be a problem, it should be easy.

And otherwise, for a person like me, I'm not a person that's really looking inside myself for strength, as far as when it comes to situations like that. It's hard, but you know, it works. From what I've learned, it works.

BROTHERHOOD

Things are changing now. I've been a Muslim for three weeks. Three weeks. What led me at first was, I can say, my whole teen life, I had been looking for a right way because I've been on the wrong path, you know, practically all my life. And now it comes to the time where I'm fed up and I don't like it and I'm not comfortable with the wrong way, I'm trying to find a right way so I can save myself, you know, I got a role model from when I came here, when I came to jail, see how the way people move, the way they talk, the way they act, the way they look out for one another.

Actually, it was like Allah pulled me towards him, he pulled me towards him because he knew the route I was going, he knows my intentions, he knows my heart, you know, so he pulled me towards him. It's like, he want me to do right, you know? It was a good feeling, it was a nice, it was a happy feeling, to know that I was being pulled by a magnificent force to do right.

When I first came in here, to be Muslim, I seen a lot of unity, a lot of brotherhood, and it made me feel good, you know, cause I don't see that nowadays, you know, brothers sticking together for what's right. I mean, that's what led me there. A lot of people, a lot of Muslims actually, they're comin' to me and putting me on about the knowledge about Mohammed, the prophet Mohammed and Allah, which is God and his prophet, they put me on about them, you know, the knowledge about them, and the way they enlightened me was the history that they gave me, the structure that they built, how the structure is now, and that's basically what enlightened me.

And the truth about right and wrong, about following the wrong path and coming to the right path, that's what enlightened me.

RAMADAN

This month is the month of Ramadan, which we fast for the sake of Allah, and also for ourselves to teach ourselves self control, self obedience, and self kindness. To keep our spirit at peace, you know, instead of in a violent form. Basically, we're doing the fast and we also have classes that teach us about other things that deal with the religion, which is Islam. Every Friday we have a service, and we have an Imam come in, which is an Islamic leader. He comes in and talks to us about other situations that we need to. How can I say it? He come in and he explain to us about what else we should be doing, as far as being a Muslim, the way we should carry ourselves. He tells us more about Islam, you know, we just sit there to listen. And then at say four o'clock on Fridays, we switch from Jumma'a to Ramadan which is fasting. We go back and take classes, studying prayers, Ha'ddiths, Sunnas. Basically we're just studying about what the prophet Mohammad had said, "Peace Be Upon Him." We follow the Koran. Hopefully we apply that to our lives as Muslims.

I mean, actually living out what you say and what you do as to follow by the Koran and Sunna. Because one thing in this religion, you have to believe in everything that's in the books, you have to believe it, because it's the truth—what's been said in the books. So by us applying it, by us living it out, we have to take that from what we read, from the book, you know, and apply it to our lives. Live it out, if we see something wrong, we correct that. Muslim should be the righteous one.

THE WRONG PATH

I'm nineteen. When I was young, I'd say when I was like twelve or thirteen, I asked myself actually, what are you doing on this path? I tried to find another path better than this. "Is this the path you want to be on?" Before I was Muslim, I was a Baptist, and honestly, the way I feel being Muslim I haven't felt when I was a Baptist. I mean, I haven't felt drawn towards it, you know. But now that I'm Muslim I feel drawn to it, I feel good about it.

The path I was on when I was thirteen, was smokin' weed, drinkin' and staying out late, not listening to my parents, getting in trouble with the cops, ya know? Well not like that. Not with the cops at this point, but just running around wild and crazy and just doing unthinkable stuff, stupid stuff that could get me in trouble, get me killed, you know. I was running with the wrong crowd at the wrong time. I wasn't thinking for myself. I was a follower at that time. I wasn't thinking for myself. I wasn't thinking about my life ahead, so that's what I consider the wrong path—staying in the dark, not being motivated to move to the light. Not doing good deeds for yourself, and for others.

At that time, I looked up to my father. But it was like, at that time, I looked up to him but I was also rebellious within myself, I didn't want to listen, I wanted to be set in my ways, do everything my way, and I had to learn the hard way. Bad role models was, you know, some of my so called friends, people I associated with, got high with, went to parties with, stood out late with. That was the bad role models that I constantly followed and followed and followed, for a couple of years

I don't have no friends now. All I have is just associates, but I won't go back to them because that's not the right way. And I know now which way it is, and being a Muslim, I will be following my brothers, you know, getting help from them, helping them out, you know, going places, doing things with them, instead of going back to the old atmosphere and environment that I used to be in. I want the way about me turning around after sacrificing my life for this situation or this cause. I'm going to be somewhere else this time, somewhere positive, nothing but positive.

SCHOOL

School was never a problem for me. It was just that I was following the wrong people at that time so. The influence of my peers was causing me to fail in class, miss school, you know, and do other things. But school was never a problem with me when I had my mind, when I was on point with things, and wasn't high. I always made sure I went to school and did what I had to do.

I was always a hard worker. I made sure I put them grades up, you know, because my father used to tell me, "The grades ain't lookin' good, you ain't getting nothing man." He stayed on top of me about my grades because it was always one issue that was always stressed in the house, so I made sure that school was a priority, a number one priority.

Horizon Academy looked into my record, my school record, my transition, and they saw that I had enough credits to get my high school diploma, I just need to pass a couple classes, get a couple credits. So I'll be able to get my high school diploma.

Moving up to eleventh grade, that's what made me happy. You know, just accomplishing being in eleventh grade, even though I knew I could have went further, but just getting to eleventh grade made me happy. You know, that I accomplished at least that, because you have some individuals that dropped out of eighth, ninth grade.

But the seniors are the ones with the bragging rights. I used to always look at them like, yeah, I'm going to be there soon, I'm going to be there real soon. Yeah, just looking at them made me work harder. But I didn't work hard enough.

THE MIND, THE STRUGGLE

I'm reading Islamic materials—things that freshen your mind. Other things will just tamper with your mind, get you back into, or try to get you back into old habits. So it will kind of decrease your faith or your focus in the religion, and to throw that off. We just have to stay with it, to stick with Islam only. No watching TV, I mean it's good to watch TV but you know, it's not good also. But we just gotta stay with Islam. That's what keeps the mind sharp and also the spirit sharp.

When Mohammed taught Islam to the people, he did go through a struggle. He went through a struggle of bringing people together, and bringing people into Islam. Having them follow by the rules and laws and commandments of Allah. We have disbelievers, and he came in and tried to bring them to be believers before it was too late. He went through a hardship with that. The strength I find in it, I'd say is by him bringing Islam to this day—to the people. Being Muslim, it strengthens me because he succeeded. He didn't give up. He kept focus at what he was supposed to do, what was meant for him to do. All across the world, you know. One man, of a kind. It is amazing, how one man can do that with the help of Allah.

SUPPORT

I'm going to be looking for a Masjed, it's a Muslim's home. And all my sisters and brothers will be there, and being those, we are one as brothers. We help one another when we're down, we strengthen when we're weak, we confront when we don't know. I'll be going to my brothers for help, and also my aunt. 'Cause she's a very strong and supportive female that's in my corner.

She always been like a mother figure to me. She always stayed on me constantly. She always supported me, financially. She just kept me with the basics—food, clothes—always kept me with talks to help me open up my mind more. That's what I mean by supportive- strong. By her standing on her toes, she kept me on my toes, you know, and kept me upfront with things.

This is where I really got in trouble with the situation that I'm in. And she's there, she's not the one to turn her back on me, she's not turning her back on me. Throughout my life certain people turned their backs on me. It didn't feel good, that's another reason why that made me turn the other way. But she's there with me, you know, strong, supportive, she's there with me. Money, clothes, you know, she's there.

She said "I love you, I miss you, can't wait 'til you come home," you know. Things of that nature. Makes me feel good.

The Imam—the leader, in Islam. He's a leader, like, he'll keep you intact with your deen, which is your knowledge and your studying of Islam, it's one main Imam which is, Imam Wali, he has been coming here so when I get home I will call him and he will um connect me with a Imam in my area which is in Queens, to help me stay on my toes, help me with whatever I need—job, schooling, housing, more knowledge—whatever it is. It's like the head leader connecting me with one of his secretaries to get me through. That's how it is.

TEMPTATION

I fear temptation. I don't want to get intact with this and then you know, the next day, I feel overwhelmed of this because of temptation, but it's also wrong. I don't want to fall off the right track just by messing with this and messing with that. I'm afraid of temptation. I fear it, because it can easily throw you off—drinking, smoking—and I know it's going to be handed to me, as a test and it's going to be my choice, my free will, my free choice. Whether I want to take that or not, you know, or continue what I'm doing that's right or continue doing what I'd been doing before. It's going to be a test for temptation

Having faith within yourself and also, the creator above, you gotta have faith within Him. I asked him to keep evil things away from me, it'll be granted but you also gotta believe within yourself that you can do it, you know, also having a strong sense of self confidence.

Yeah, actually it is, I mean, the three main things that I'm mostly going to have to do—or any religious person is going to have to do—is he have to be mentally, physically, and spiritually strong. Working out, stay on top of his reading. Keeping his spirit strong, and also the mind, you know. Those are the main things that I have to do. You can't eat certain things. Pork, we can't eat. That is not permissible for us. As Muslims, we're given a document stating all the things we're supposed to eat and not eat. So basically, we eat chicken, we eat vegetables, stuff like that. Fruits. Keeping yourself healthy, but nothing hiram, which is swine, pork. The only time we can eat pork is when there is nothing left in the house for us to eat and pork is just the only thing laying around. We're not allowed to eat all of it, just, I can say, just one-third of that, just a little piece to satisfy our hunger.

STAYING ON TRACK

From what I'm looking at and I see what' happening in my life situation, things fall in place for a certain reason, I'd say it's going right, all I just needed was just a push and a little guidance, and I found that. I just gotta use it to the best of my abilities when I get home, and I feel like it won't be a hard task to do. I feel like it'll be something very easy to do, to stay on track.

I'm gonna go to college. Before I got locked up, I was in the T.C.I., something like a trade school. I'll get back into a program and stay in contact with my Muslim brothers. Then when I get another chance, I'm going to get an associates degree, and then afterwards, you know, once I get settled in financially I'll take up another trade, electrical technician, or psychology, or something else.

When I get home, before I have a job placement, one of my brothers is going to help me. He's going to help me with construction, help me get set with construction, just to get me on a foot, teach me. 'Cause he asked me if I knew anything about it, I said it shouldn't be hard. I'm a fast learner. All you gotta do is show me once or twice. After that, there should be no problem. He's a contractor, and he's going to help me get on, get straight. So I take that as one sign, one step of my life that's already put into place. That's already going to start off right. And as I continue from there, other things will gradually develop and attach to whatever I'm doing in my life. Good things, I feel that coming. I'll continue. This is just patience, motivation, and willingness. Everything will be all right.

Caught Up

Kavon

I'm from the Virgin Islands. The way our parents raise kids is different. They raise kids with discipline. School. You go home, they don't ask you, "Did you do your homework?" and this and that. But if you did something bad, you're going to get dealt with. All the good stuff… brush it off. My grandmother's old, my mother passed away. You know, our father was never there, so it's like we look at our grandmother and she'd just be pushing discipline, discipline. Really.

You don't have nothing school-wise. You don't have nobody at home to tutor you. But my uncle, he's working. He'd come home at eleven. By the time he come at eleven, you're getting ready for school in the morning. So you don't have nobody to tutor you, or help you—get you prepared for your test on Friday. You know what I mean? Stuff like that. Like a normal kid.

I have a little sister. She's fifteen. She's having a baby. She's due any day now. My whole family's looking at her like they don't want nothing to do with her, but me I really do. I'm not mad that she's pregnant. I can't do nothing about it. Everybody's neglecting her, don't want her around and stuff. She's young. When I come out I plan to do something very smart. Not even with drugs or nothing. So when I'm in here I'm going to try and get my G.E.D., so that when I get out there, I can start on step two, instead of trying to do step one and two.

My little sister. I really really feel for her. I haven't spoke to her since I was out there. And I really, really want to speak to her. My family's not… the best—they're not good at all. They raised on this West Indian attitude, you know. Discipline, discipline. My little sister's just out there, going from my grandmother house to her boyfriend house. And her boyfriend is my age—her baby father's my age. I've never met him.

I spoke to my sister, and I made her come home. Come home, you know. I took her up to get something to eat. We sat. We talked. She was telling me that, "I can't stay. Mom's making me stressed out. She doing this and that." I didn't know she was pregnant that whole time. So we talking, and I'm like "you know, you can't keep running away. You're going to have her worried. And something's going to happen to her, or something'll happen to you. Or you're going to get put away, and nobody gonna take it." So she was like, "Yeah, you right." That's my grandmother's heart, really.

I gave her some money, and she went. Stayed there for about two days and she ran away again. Came back one time before I got arrested. There was a rumor she was pregnant. When I got in here, I called one time, and I spoke to her. She was like three months. And that was a long time ago. I'm like, "Wow." She's supposed to be due next month. Definitely next month she's supposed to be due. I told my girlfriend to make sure she gets a picture of the baby. Find out the name, and all that. She having a little girl, too.

I believe she don't have no help, and that's the whole thing. I know the guy's my age, but I know the role. He not doing nothing; ain't nothing going to get done. I don't want them to raise the baby on drugs. Off of drug money, you know what I'm sayin'? He's out there selling to make sure the baby have pampers. I can't do that no more.

I'm serious about raising my little niece the right way. The way my sister ain't been raised and I wasn't raised—a whole bunch of different ways to go around that. I don't even know where to start right there, you know, with my sister, my little sister… You've got to start somewhere. That's my main goal, too. To show her right from wrong... Things that I didn't learn, my sister didn't learn. Really she didn't even live her teenager life. She's only fifteen.

I remember when she was born, my mother was holding on her hand. You know, "Here go your little sister," and she puts out her hand. And I was bugging, like, "oh my g"—she was so small. I'm like, "Oh my god. A little baby. She's small!" You know, I was holding her like a brother. And when she got older she was just like, a brat. You know, she'd do things and get away with it. Like everything she'd do, my grandmother was on her side. You can't say nothing to her without you getting in trouble by my grandmother. But my grandma was always like, "Yo, this little girl." I used to always tell my grandmother, "You think I'm bad? Watch my sister." And she'd always be like, "She's not doing nothing." She never believed me.

Now she's going to do it now. I spoke to her, and she's like, "I need help with your sister. I can't deal with her. This little girl driving me crazy." You know, and I didn't want to say, "I told you so." But I just keep my mouth shut, like, "Yeah?" I never get a chance to speak to her though.

The last time I saw her was the summertime. And she was telling me, you know, "Aw, man. I'm pregnant." And I was like, "So where you stay?" And she was like "Yeah, but then I leave and I go to my boyfriend house." And you know, it just sounded so funny to hear her say that. Like, "My god. Her babyfather house. This is crazy. It's real." I'm not used to it.

My girlfriend said she saw her in August, and she was big. You know, so I'm like, "Did you see her boyfriend?" She said "Yeah. He don't look too bright." So I'm like, damn. I already know, I got my mind set that he's not doing nothing. That's it. I'm going to have to play a major part I her life, in her little baby life....

The things that didn't go right for me, I want to go right for her. Family support is a big part—plays a big part. I know all about it. 'Cause if somebody ain't going to show you the right thing, you ain't going to know nothing about the right—it's not going to exist in your mind, like, "This is what I got to do. I have to come home." Maybe read a book before I watch TV, or maybe just sit down and give the homework two hours and put the effort in it. I think it's starting with the parents. If you don't pay attention, kids going to do whatever. And the neighborhood we in, it's always negative. It's always right there, so it's easy to be negative—for things to go this way, instead of going that way.

Now I'm just focused on my little sister. I wish I could speak to her, or get in touch with her, but it's hard. She's on the run, but pregnant on the run, fifteen, there's so much stress. My family, instead of them helping her, it's just, "She out of control. She out of control." I know she's out of control, but I look at the big picture now. It's done. There's nothing you can do.

I wanted a kid so bad, but my girlfriend was telling me we ain't ready.

And I was like, "How we ain't ready? How we ain't ready?" No I see how we ain't ready. It's just things like this. I'd have been in here, and she'd have been pregnant out there by her self. That'd hurt me even more. So this is my last stop, right here. I ain't coming back here.

My girlfriend was like, "You can't keep living like this." You know, I've got a whole bunch of stuff ahead. I've got my sister, my girlfriend. And I've got her family—you know, I told that I'm not coming back to jail. And I disappointed them. So now I have to them that I'm a changed. person. I'm not going to come back to jail. When I come out I'm going to be doing something that keep me from coming back in here.

If I'm really serious about it, I'll do it. I think this is the best time to do it now. Start now. Don't wait until I get out there, then start.

BEGINNING OF THE BOOK

When I was younger, I say... twelve... I used to go to school. I'd rush to do my homework, just to get outside, go with my friends, to go in the back and sell drugs. So it wasn't like I was really into school, because I was into selling drugs. I was addicted to it. I was addicted to making sales. I got arrested at fourteen; I got arrested for making a sale. And when I came out, I did a robbery. I was just around the wrong crowd. I got caught up. They let me back out, and I got caught for another sale. They sent me upstate. They sent me upstate for eighteen months, and I ended up doing two years for that. So when I was upstate, they had school, but it wasn't—you know, I was still like, "When I get out, I've got my mind set. I'm going to save my money. I'm not going to sell to nobody I don't know." So the drug thing was still in my mind. When I was out there, I'd hear my older cousin, he wasn't into drugs. But they used to say, Navon is the youngest brother and Kavon is the oldest brother. Kavon is like reckless. I was reckless. I used to go out there and just do stupid stuff, and not even think about what I was doing. So, like, at twelve, I used to go to school. You know, I would sit there, do work, somebody would make a joke. I used to get up and react. By hitting them. I'd get suspended for a week. You know, thinking it's good, but really it's hurting me. And then I'd come back and they're on chapter two. And I'm still on the beginning of the book.

I met a kid in my school and the only reason to go to school was just to meet him. When I would go to his house, it was just like the pharmacy. His father had a basement full of everything. Weed....

I was about twelve. I met him in school. Not to say that he wasn't in here too—come in here, and we'd be sitting. And I had thought about it, like this is a rerun. We was doing that when we was young. And now we're here. And we're still close. Not that I cut him off. We used to go to his house, and he used to keep lookout, make sure you know—'cause his moms used to come home from work. He used to give me stuff, and I used to take it back, and I used to go handle it, and he came to school the next day and split it, like this and that. Like, damn, "this is my best friend now." He always had a scam. Always. Always something. He used to be teaching me how to bend the metrocards, and just keep swiping them and swiping them all day. And it's like, "Wow you swipe your people in for a dollar a swipe." Bending metrocards. I'm like, "This kid is a real hustler." He became my friend.

And then I seen him in here, it was like, "Wow." It's another thing that makes me think. I see all my childhood friends. And I see them in here. Like I seen another one up on the bus, that was there for murder. And two attempts. And he was saying, give him my number, so he could write me. And I had a pen in my pocket. And I was like, "I don't have a pen." You know. It's just not the same anymore. Those aren't your friends no more. That's what always pulled me back down.

I had teachers that liked me, and wanted to work with me, but my mind wasn't focused on school. Now that I think about it, if I had used it, I'd probably be in college right now, probably playing ball. I had teachers that was willing to work with me, but I just loved the drugs.

I had a teacher that was calling my house. And that was elementary. Her name was Velazquez. I had to be ten, ten or eleven. Not too sure. I went to junior high school. She said she saw something in me nobody else saw. I didn't even see it, though. But she said she seen something. Potential. When I wanted to learn something, I'd put my mind to it and do it. But it was so much things distracting me, I couldn't get my mind focused on school. I wasn't worrying about school.

Ms. Velasquez. I remember her, I drove her crazy. I know I used to see her when I was out there too. The school was right there and the pizza shop was over here. I used to be in the pizza shop, you know, doing what I was doing. And she'd come in and say, "What you doing? Why you not in school with us?" I had a crackhead sitting on the bench and she really knew what was going on. "You can't be doing that. You've got to change your life!" I was like,

"You don't remember me." She said, "How could I forget you?" I said, "What's my name?" She said my whole name and I was like, wow. She still remembered me. There's something about me that she remembered.

I had a lot of people that cared for me too. Another teacher named Mr. Stewart. He came and he told me—he used to joke with me, then he used to be serious. I was cool with him, joking, he'd tell me and I'd listen to him. I listened to him and I said, "Yeah, you know, I'm not going to do that." You know, look at all the other kids that's in school, half of them was in jail. I'm like "Nah, I'm not going to go to jail."

I went to jail. From jail they put me in Brandeis, I was in Brandeis for about two months, and it didn't last — I was in a gang. And I was at the school, it was like, "Who's the new kid?" And kids was like askin' me stuff and I'm trying to tell them I just came from upstate. So now they following me, so if something happened, they're looking for me to help them, or me to be a part of it. And silly old me fell right into it. I started fighting. They threw me out the school. And I signed up for a G.E.D. school, and it was like, when I'm going there, my phone would ring, and it would be a sale, and I would be like, "It's over for school. I've got to do what I've got to do." You know, I don't need school because I'm getting money. That's how I see it. That's how a lot of people see it too, now that I think about it.

Only two people out of my crew got a G.E.D. and a high school diploma. My girlfriend was the one to motivate me. Everyday I'd call her in the morning and speak to her and she'd ask me how I'm doing in school; what I'm doing, what I'm up to. So I'd try to keep up. I don't sit out there and be like no night guard, no TV, I'd go and read and write. I try to keep my mind focused. When I go out there, I don't want to go backward, I want to go forward. I always been going backwards.

I'm not a follower. I'm always a leader, but they look up to me and it's like, I've got to live that image. I'm a leader. I'm a leader. You know, being a leader is a lot. You can't be a leader and just sit back. You've got to get up and do something sometimes. You've got to make it happen, and make them believe you're a leader. The leader thing is not always good. Even being a follower, they can use you.

TO BE A LEADER

A leader. If you're looking up to me, and I'm the leader, I've got to set an example for you. It can be a positive or negative example. If I'm going to finish school, you know, then you probably be following the positive. Now a leader that got a fancy car, some clothes, then you're going to want to be just like me. I'd like to follow the leader that finished school in high school. My girlfriend finished school, got a job, had a life. My cousin, negative followed that. He'd sell drugs. He got shot; he got this and that. He's in and out of jail. It's like two leaders.

Two different leaders. Two different leaders, positive and negative. I've been doing the negative all my life. I'm going to try the positive—trying to be positive, try to do the positive.

My girlfriend, Mara, she's a leader and she don't know. Another thing I like about her is she honest. She always tell me "All you have is your word. If you don't have your word, you don't have nothing." I always remember that. I ain't never forget that. She used to tell me that a lot. I use that, sometimes, when I'm talking to people. I tell them, "All you got is your word. If you don't got your word, you don't have nothing." So that's one of my main words right there, and, I love her a lot.

I met my girlfriend at thirteen, but we got stronger when I was in there, you know, writing her. I had a clear mind. I'd talk to her, she'd talk back to me. Understand that I wanted to change. I met her at her party. One time, there was a party in her house. I went over there, and—you know, I'd been seeing her before, used to be seeing her on the street, but I never paid her no mind. One day one of my friends was going out with her sister, and I hooked up with her from that. We just never broke up from there. And you know, when I was upstate, that love was always still in. A couple of years. We ain't even married. But that's going to be my wife.

I see myself as a leader. When I put my mind to something, I can do anything. I know I can. I can play basketball. When I was young I could play basketball. I was nice on the block. And then when I'd get in front of a bunch of people, I'd freeze up. And then I'd start going to parks. Some people would come and they would have next, then other people would come and they would have next. I'd play. I'd play. You know, people have next. You know, they'd come with they five. And after them, the people after them got next, so it was ten. Fifteen, twenty. Now you have twenty people watching you play, and ten on the court. Now I'm playing. I'm doing my thing. I'm breaking my shyness, things like that.

That's another thing. I'm known for playing basketball, fighting. I'm known where I am. So I have to keep that image up, sometimes. Sometimes they'd be like—I know, one of my friends would say, "Oh yeah, Kay you're getting soft." I'm not getting soft, I'm getting older now. Things ain't going going to the precinct when not more. When you go to the precinct and get fingerprinted, what are you going to do?

So I started using my head a lot.

Now I'm thinkin' about my niece, and how I can be an uncle-slash-godfather, stepfather. All that. Everything that she needs. That's why when I get done I'm going to get a job, so when I come out... I can get my G.E.D. so when I come out, I can get a job. And when it's time for her to go to school, and she need a school dress, her cap and dress, I can tell her, show her the right way. Like my sister, she got her whole life ahead of her—tell her she got to go to school, too. If she go to school, she need a babysitter. If I'm not working, I can do it. I can provide for the babysitter.

I live with my girlfriend—and I've got a cousin that got a house but I really don't—I'm not going to stay over there, because I don't want to smoke or nothing. I'm serious about that. I'm gonna eliminate it and stay away from it, period. I'm really, really focused this time, not like before, when I went up as an adolescent. I wasn't really, really focused, for two years I was up there, it was just "I can't wait until I get out there." Now I can wait. I'm not really pressured. I'm not planning to do nothing. And that's what I realized when I was up there—I didn't really do nothing when I was up there. I didn't get no G.E.D., I didn't step up in my academics or nothing. I was in a rush just to get into the streets. I'm not in a rush right now.

I'm trying to get something done while I'm here, eliminate step one so I can go to step two. And from step two I go to three.

STRIVE

I was working for a pharmacy. I was delivering medicine to people's house. But they fired me, because I had drug charge. The drug charge and the medicine don't go together, they said. So... They had to let me go. I was making good money, too.

I was thinking about going to Strive. The director was in here. He knew my family. So he provide for you even if you've got a felony. They've got job placement, help you with résumés—a whole bunch of stuff that's behind it.

And, I did it before—I tried to do it before, but I wasn't really serious with myself. I went in there, and everybody had suits on, and I had on street clothes. Everybody's standing up and they said, "If you've got a suit on and you're properly dressed, sit down." And it was 64 people in there. Me included, 65. Everybody sat down except for me. I've got on jeans, a regular shirt, with some sneakers. And they've got shoes and slacks on. It's like, "You don't belong here." I was like, "Yeah, I don't belong here," and I cursed them out and I left.

I thought about it, "Wow." I should've used that when I was out there. I probably wouldn't be here now. They got lifetime job service. They'll always—if there's a job open, they'll recommend you and give you support, call for references. I know one friend that went through it, and he got a job and all that. He's doing good. I'd go back there now, with a different attitude, though. A different person. They wouldn't recognize me if I go in there the way I am now. I'm serious about changing. I've got goals.

I want to do something like maintenance. Like when I was in D.F.Y. I did pick up a trade. I was doing maintenance—I was cleaning carpets, I was painting. You know, maintenance jobs. I really liked it. I was into it, and I know I could do it. If you really want to do it. If you really want to become something, and you're going to do it, make sure nothing pulls you down or holds you back.

For me, I think what holds me back is just the whole family thing. I

didn't have that family love and support. I had a couple of family members that really wanted me to do good, and really believed in me. And then I had my grandmother saying that, "Oh you're just going to be a bad boy." When I was born, my mother brought me in the house, and she said that—you know—my uncle used to always tell me that my grandfather looked at me and said, "He's going to be a bad boy." I used to always think about that, like "Damn." So it really hit me, now that my grandfather passed away. The only thing he knows is that I am a bad boy. I don't want people to always think that. "Oh, Kay the bad boy." I got a aunt that, that's what she called me. She probably ain't even know my real name.

I don't care what people think about me now. And that's how I know I've changed. 'Cause before, I always did. That's what my girl used to always say, "You worry about what people say, I don't." That's one thing that I really learned. I don't worry about what people say no more and how they think about me. As long as I know what I'm doing, what I have to do and I'm making the person I gotta make happy happy, you know. I have a girlfriend that's willing to work with me, through all of this. She's working. She's a secretary and she's in college right now. So she's ahead of me... Way ahead of me. But she's willing to work with me. I'm just not trying to let nobody down no more. My whole life was a promise.

No matter what, I'm gonna strive.